Reverse Mortgage 360

A New Perspective

For information, please contact:

Jim Hostler
Phone: 928.225.7418
Email: Jim@reversemortgage360.org
Website: **ReverseMortgage360.org**
Facebook:
https://www.facebook.com/reversemortgage360

Legal Disclaimer

I have written this book to be an educational guide on reverse mortgages. The opinions expressed are solely my own. While best efforts have been made in preparing this book, I make no representations or warranties of any kind and assume no liabilities of any kind with respect to the accuracy or completeness of the contents of this book. I have also referenced the most recent underwriting guidelines at the time the book was written; however, in no manner is anything implied for any offer to lend or that any material and/or information found in this book should be used in lieu of current HUD HECM underwriting guidelines. As with all financial decisions, appropriate professional counsel should always be sought, along with sufficient education on the HECM product. The author shall not be held liable or responsible to any person or entity with respect to any loss or incidental or consequential damages caused, or alleged to have been caused, directly or indirectly, from the information or programs contained herein.

All educational materials used in this book are not endorsed by nor approved by HUD, FHA, or any other company, person, or entity. Portions of federal guidelines have been referenced in this book for educational purposes. Relevant regulations should always be read and understood in full when needed.

Table of Contents

PART THREE: More Things I Need to Know

PART FOUR: GLOSSARY

Foreword

Jim Hostler has become a friend and inspiration to me, and I have been in the mortgage industry for over 20 years! In **Reverse Mortgage 360, A New Perspective**, Jim has provided education, insight, and information in a straightforward manner based on real life experiences. His interactions with real estate and financial services professionals give the reader an opportunity to view HECM loans in a more unbiased manner. Jim has expertly woven his knowledge of the HECM mortgage product within real life scenarios. His passion for sharing the merits of HECMs while not shoving it down our throats is both admirable and reassuring. This is real world, down to earth sentiments from someone who has experience and compassion for those he serves in the mortgage industry. I recommend this book to anyone who is even slightly interested in learning more about HECM loans.

Timothy Parker
Account Executive
November 2017
Edmonds, WA
25+ Years in the Mortgage Industry

Endorsements

"As a Seniors Real Estate Specialist in Arizona, I have worked with Jim Hostler for many years. I am thrilled to recommend his book: "Reverse Mortgage 360 – A New Perspective". It provides a road map with a proven strategy for creating a meaningful balanced life without stress. Jim is committed to his clients, truly caring, and he connects to improve the quality of the lives they are living. A must read for seniors, it could set you free."

Brenda Powell, Realtor, SRES, GRI, ABR, CRS
HomeSmart Real Estate

"Honestly, there is no author who knows more about reverse mortgages than Jim! Read his book and follow the steps to assist your senior clients. It is about time for this book to arrive in every Realtor's library. A MUST read!"

Sandra Anselmo. Associate Broker
Redstone Properties, Sedona, AZ.

"Jim helped me tremendously on a reverse mortgage on my home. Anytime I have any questions I can contact Jim and he will assist me. I would recommend him to anyone that wants to do a reverse mortgage on their home. In my opinion he is very trustworthy and if I was in a position to get another home Jim would be number one on my list."

Sandra Hall
client

"Jim Hostler offers practical guidance for those who want to enjoy a mortgage free retirement. By following his recommendations, we significantly improved our credit ratings, obtained a reverse mortgage on our home and have a line of credit as a nest egg. Now we feel more confident about our retirement future!"

Cal & Cheryl
clients

"My husband and I were very pleased with Jim as our agent to procure a reverse mortgage. He handled the many issues that arose with a calm and cheerful demeanor and always responded to our concerns. His sense of humor and ready smile make it all ever so much easier."

Nancy Norman McLaughlin
client

"I was initially impressed with Jim Hostler's enthusiasm, communication skills, and professional demeanor. With the knowledge that I have gained I feel confident that the [retirement] path will be easier to travel."

Ronda Straten
client

Introduction

Reverse mortgages aren't the mortgages they were only a few years ago. Because of the financial meltdown the U.S. experienced between 2008 and 2012, HUD looked at the then-existing reverse mortgage program and, beginning in 2012 through 2017, has made substantial changes to the program. These major changes within the last several years give cause as to why reverse mortgage professionals have an obligation to educate consumers, their families, and other professionals.

I have found the clear majority of people have beliefs about the reverse mortgage program that today are simply not true and are based on hearsay or reverse mortgages of long ago. Subsequently, *the largest challenge facing the industry today is education.* The educational process isn't only about educating senior homeowners who may benefit from a reverse mortgage: it is also about educating their families and the professionals who serve and support seniors.

I feel my most important job today as a reverse mortgage specialist is to be a *reverse mortgage educator.* Again, there have been and continue to be changes to the program. The product wasn't a good product when it first came out, giving cause to the myths and misconceptions of today.

And the education needs to go out beyond the senior homeowner. A diverse group of professionals, including financial advisors, real estate agents, insurance agents, accountants, and senior care professionals (to name but a few), all work with and support seniors. Subsequently, they can often refer their senior clientele to a reverse mortgage specialist to help that senior. But this diverse group of professionals needs to know, at least at a high level, accurate information about today's reverse mortgage.

Let's look at my own profession, mortgage banking. Reverse mortgages are significantly different than a traditional forward mortgage, and as such they need to be viewed as a profession within a profession. The mortgage professionals selling reverse mortgages need to be educated in them and work with them full-time. And with all due respect to traditional forward mortgage professionals, I strongly don't recommend working with a mortgage professional who isn't a full-time reverse mortgage specialist. Let me say this a little differently: it is my strong belief that any person who hasn't *studied* reverse mortgages since 2015, and *continues to study them*, doesn't know today's reverse mortgage... period.

Reverse mortgages were seen for years as a loan of last resort. When homeowners had run out of money and exhausted all other means to support themselves, only then was a reverse mortgage considered. Additionally, there was virtually no qualifying needed other than the equity in the home. All of this has changed and continues to change. This is my purpose in writing this book: to provide an informative book that educates people in today's reverse mortgage, thereby giving them a new (and accurate) perspective of the features and benefits of today's HECM. Today, HECMs are being recognized for what they are: **a retirement planning tool.** In fact, "new academic research demonstrates how HECMs can play a vital role in retirement planning–not just as a tool of last resort, but as a

---

[1] Salter, Pfeiffer and Evensky, Texas Tech University, "Standby Reverse Mortgages: A Risk Management Tool for Retirement," Journal of Financial Planning, 2012.

strategic way to provide greater financial flexibility to seniors with ample savings."[1]

In addition to the senior homeowner looking to obtain a reverse mortgage, often it is important for their children to understand how today's reverse mortgage works. There are two main reasons for children, or at least one child, in the family to be educated in today's reverse mortgages. First, when their parent(s) consider taking out a reverse mortgage, if the children are educated in reverse mortgages they can be another set of eyes and ears in the decision-making process. The children are the people the parents trust the most (generally speaking) and as such if a family can discuss this together they can make an educated decision on whether or not to proceed with a reverse mortgage. The second reason for the children to understand the basics of a reverse mortgage is that when Mom and Dad no longer live in the home, the children know their options in advance of a life changing event.

I have also consulted with single seniors who often have family or friends whom they trust and want them to sit in on their initial presentation to help them better understand how a reverse mortgage works and to see if it is in their best interest to obtain one. I always encourage this and see it with the same benefits of having the child of a senior participating in a presentation.

The final group of people that need to be educated in how a reverse mortgage works are what I call *senior supporting professionals*. This includes real estate agents, financial advisors, attorneys, senior care professionals, CPA's, accountants, personal bankers, insurance agents, and mortgage professionals. I believe that today the vast majority of these professionals do not have an accurate and basic understanding of today's reverse mortgage. And why this is so important? Because their clients trust them to guide and inform them as to what is in their best interest. And if their trusted advisor isn't educated at least enough to know to look into a reverse mortgage, and instead recommends something different, the trusted advisor may, in fact, may not be giving the best advise to their senior client.

I have been in the mortgage industry for almost 30 years and about three years ago I got introduced to reverse mortgages. I have invested a great deal of time educating myself and speaking to and learning from other reverse mortgage professionals. I finally feel confident and knowledgeable enough to call myself a reverse mortgage specialist. And as a reverse mortgage specialist, I am engaged daily in conversations with seniors, their families or trusted friends, and a diverse group of senior supporting professionals. I see first-hand how much education and a new perspective on today's reverse mortgage is needed such that it will allow potentially millions of seniors, their families, and respective senior supporting professionals to make informed and educated choices with today's reverse mortgage. And to know that today's HECMs are now a retirement planning tool and not a loan of last resort. To this vision, I dedicate this book.

PART ONE

Advice for You, You & You

CHAPTER ONE

Advice to Begin With

Ah… reverse mortgages: "Run from them," "Don't ever do it!", "They cost too much," "They're a bad deal," "You'll lose your home" … and the list goes on. I want to give some advice to three groups of people:

The borrowers, the person or couple who qualifies for and is looking to obtain or is interested in a reverse mortgage.

The second group is *the borrower's family and friends.* This is a group whom borrowers trust which are often involved with the decision-making process of the borrowers obtaining a reverse mortgage.

And I also want to include a group I call *the senior supporting professionals.* A senior supporting professional is anyone who professionally is in a position to work with and/or support the senior population. This third group includes financial advisors, real estate agents, home builders, accountants, CPAs, fiduciaries, insurance agents, attorney's, bankers, and the senior care professionals such as care agencies, social workers, and geriatric care managers. And for all three of these groups, I want to offer some advice up front, a new perspective, in how to embark on the decision of getting a reverse mortgage or supporting someone getting a reverse mortgage.

The first reverse mortgage was in 1961. That is a long time ago in the lifetime of a financial product. Over this long history a lot has changed, with the most recent change occurring October 2, 2017. I share how long reverse mortgages have been around because (as with anything that has a long history), people have formed opinions about the product, deservingly or not. And with opinions comes a sense of knowing. When you form an opinion about something, you think you know something about it. And human nature being what it is, if anyone wants to challenge your opinion, most likely you will dig in your heels and defend your opinion… because *you* know, right?

This isn't about right or wrong, but rather about bringing awareness to an issue. And concerning this issue, reverse mortgages, I want to bring awareness to three groups of people before we even start down the rabbit hole of discussing reverse mortgages. However, before we begin our journey, I invite you to put your opinions aside. You have opinions, own your opinions, and no one is taking them away from you. But *so much has changed with reverse mortgages in recent years* that if you haven't *studied* them since 2015, I guarantee *at least* one thing you know about them is wrong.

Some advice for the first group, the senior homeowner considering a reverse mortgage. Congratulations on being open and looking into a reverse mortgage. You're embarking on a journey unlike anything you have ever done. And the reason I say this is because for our entire life, we (as a society) are taught to get a traditional forward, often 30-year fixed rate mortgage, and then work to pay it off. End of story. This is *not* how a reverse mortgage works. But a reverse mortgage is a critical decision in your life because you could end up having it longer than a 30-year mortgage! To start, I invite you to create a notebook and consciously take on learning about reverse mortgages and *how one can be of benefit to you!*

On the first page of your new notebook, write out, "Why do I want or need a reverse mortgage?" This keeps you focused on learning and knowing what you need to know. It also prevents you from going off course into information that may simply not be applicable for you. This also creates the next reason I recommend having your notebook, for the questions you have and *will have*.

In the next section of your notebook, create a section for questions and begin now by taking time to write out all the questions you already have. And keep this section "live", meaning today you don't or won't know what or all the questions to even ask. As you educate yourself more and meet with a reverse mortgage specialist to go over your initial figures, you will see the ways a reverse mortgage may be able to be structured to benefit you... and I guarantee new questions will come up. It will also prepare you better, if you proceed with a reverse mortgage, for your counseling session that is required. Having this notebook will also serve you for years to come as a reference for your reverse mortgage.

Another section I strongly encourage, if you don't have one already, is a budget. One powerful example I can share about the benefits of creating a budget is of a couple I know who made a good living. The husband was earning about $100,000 a year and they were very comfortable. I know this because I did their loan for them about four years ago when they bought their home.

Fast forward to a few months ago and I received a call from a financial advisor I know. She asked me to meet with one of her clients to discuss them getting a reverse mortgage. "Why, what was their story?" I asked myself, as it was the couple for whom I did their purchase transaction about four years ago! It turns out they were spending like he was still making the 100 grand and not based on their retirement income. Said differently, they were spending at a rate where they would be out of money long before the mortality tables said they would still be around.

Again, reverse mortgages require a new perspective of understanding. And if you were to save every piece of paper from when you started considering a reverse mortgage until you close on yours, you will have over 500 pages of documents. Don't freak out on me, just know this is the world of mortgages today for both traditional forward and reverse mortgages.

You will be given copies of everything, and at the least you need to keep copies of the three pages of your "initial figures": *the amortization schedule, reverse mortgage comparison, and total annual loan cost.* These will be included in your final closing package, but I always recommend keeping the initial ones as virtually every time the figures will change from the initial ones to the final ones. Which brings me to another item I recommend keeping: *a copy of your closing documents.* The title/escrow company will give you copies of all the documents you sign at your closing—this is the package I am speaking about.

The bottom-line piece of advice, and in my opinion the best piece of advice anyone can give you regarding getting a reverse mortgage, is education, education, education. I am not saying be a financial expert. But what I am saying is reverse mortgages are unique and need a new perspective of financial education to understand them. Educate yourself. The web is full of information. HUD and AARP are two good sources. Additionally, my website, www.reversemortgage360.org, is a dynamic site with information on reverse mortgages and issues of interest to seniors. And, finally, talk to others… but with a HUGE word of caution. If your friends can't balance a check book, don't seek their financial advice on a reverse mortgage. *If a trusted professional has not educated themselves on today's reverse mortgage, don't take their advice, period.*

Which leads me to my advice about family and friends. The husband of a client of mine passed away unexpectedly. She decided she wanted a reverse mortgage. When I met with her, her brother-in-law was there, too. He was a former chief financial officer of a bank. It was great, as he was financially more educated than I am. But I was the reverse mortgage expert. We respected each other's "turf" and had a great conversation. Again, given his financial background, he was financially very savvy. But he also learned things from me about a reverse mortgage. In the end, she proceeded with a reverse mortgage. It was in her best interest and helped her, and all of us could see and agreed on that.

This is a rather extreme example of a friend or family member's knowledge and of someone you would have available and trust in helping you make a decision. Conversely, if you have a family or friend and you want them to be part of the decision-making process, yet they can't balance a checkbook (true story, as I know people that can't), please don't ask them for financial advice!

Child(ren) of parent(s) are often involved with their parent(s) in the decision-making process, too. Personally, I believe it is great to have at least one child who can be with Mom and Dad (or single parent) in the decision-making part of deciding if it is in Mom and Dad's best interest to obtain a reverse mortgage. And I say this for a couple reasons.

First, after the borrower has met with the reverse mortgage specialist, if the son or daughter is also part of the initial presentation, they too are educated in the reverse mortgage and can help clarify or answer any questions that might come up. Or clarify the issue such that relevant, specific question(s) can be asked of the reverse mortgage specialist. Keep in mind, and I share more later in this book, children of parent(s) getting a reverse mortgage can also be part of the counseling. Again, helping everyone to be informed and educated.

The second reason it is often good for a son or daughter to be part of the decision-making process is that they are the ones who will be heirs and must handle the estate. Knowing not only that there is a reverse mortgage on Mom and Dad's home, but also the options at the time the home is no longer the primary residence, is certainly something to know and plan for ahead of time, rather than reacting at the moment of grief and the loss of a parent.

I also want to speak directly with the family or friend who is asked to be a consultant for the borrower looking to possibly get a reverse mortgage. Everyone has skills and talents, and if your skill or talent isn't finance, please don't enter the scene as a confidant for the borrower. I see this, in my opinion, too frequently. The family or friend knows very little about finance, and yet they're invited into the conversation about the borrower getting the reverse mortgage.

It may seem like I am talking out of both sides of my mouth now, but I always encourage everyone to know more about reverse mortgages. So, if the family or friend is truly open to being educated, to know more, great, join in the conversation. But at the end of the day, trust your decision on a professional who knows the business of reverse mortgages. You most likely don't go to the doctor with a family member or friend and after the doctor renders her/his advice, consult with the family or friend for advice on what is best for you. Let me sum it up by saying it differently.

I always encourage a team approach to reverse mortgages, if applicable. For example, a couple may be just fine making the decision on their own… many are. But when it is decision time, give the most amount of weight to the professional giving the advice. If you're not comfortable with their advice, seek another professional with whom you are comfortable. Remember, job one: education!

Which brings me to the third group that is very often involved in the decision-making process of a borrower obtaining a reverse mortgage: senior supporting professionals. I believe I could almost dedicate the entire book to this subject, as it is so broad in scope. However, I am going to keep it high level, and given my advice, I believe it is applicable to any senior serving professional with whom you may work.

So, who are these people, senior serving professionals? I am going to define them as *potentially anyone who works in a profession that serves the senior market.* Can't get much wider of a brush stoke than that, can you? Specifically, there are several professions that come to mind, and in fairness let me call out my own to start: the mortgage bankers.

Generally speaking, the professionals working within the mortgage banker's profession know a crazy amount about traditional forward mortgages. But a reverse mortgage, while it is also a mortgage, is hardly anything like a forward mortgage. And for that one seemingly simple reason, if the mortgage banker you choose to deal with is not a reverse mortgage specialist, I would suggest finding one who is. With a reverse mortgage, a traditional forward mortgage professional could give all-meaning good advice that can, in fact, be the *wrong advice*. If I sound like I am "harping" on this one, I own it. Deal with a professional reverse mortgage specialist.

Regarding all of the senior supporting professions, if the professionals within their respective profession knew just a little about a reverse mortgage, they would be able to potentially know when to reach out to a reverse mortgage specialist. But this is a two-way street! The reverse mortgage specialist needs to know at least a little about these professions, such that if we see a need we'll know who to potentially reach out to across different professions to best serve a senior. I know a lot of this occurs, and I not only support that but encourage all professionals to cooperate and collaborate to help the seniors.

That said, all professionals have their profession. Sounds basic, simple, and common sense, but I have seen too much of the downside of this already to not make a point here. I once had a potential client who was researching whether a reverse mortgage would be good for him and his wife. He was about 14 years older than his wife. I spoke at length with him to help him understand it and felt that after a couple good meetings he had a good handle on reverse mortgages. He was telling me how different features worked, which reinforced, to me, that he was "getting it." He wanted me to go talk to his "financial advisor", which I did, and the financial advisor and I had a great conversation about the city, history, what he did, and other trivial things I don't recall. But what was missing? The "financial advisor" had his own opinions and wasn't open to anything new or anything I had to say. Can you say, "deal dead?" And it was very possible that obtaining a reverse mortgage was in the best interest of our mutual client. More needed to be explored, but the rest of the story we shall never know as an ignorant person stopped that conversation before it could be had.

You don't bring your friend who is a wiz with computers to your annual income tax meeting with your accountant and take the advice of your friend over your accountant, right? So, don't take the advice of a professional who is not a reverse mortgage professional as the "best or final advice".

I want to extend an invitation to all senior supporting professionals. Reach out to a reverse mortgage specialist and get educated on today's reverse mortgage. You don't and shouldn't become an expert, but rather have a basic understanding of what they are such that in the event you come across a senior who may benefit from a reverse mortgage, you would know to refer them to a reverse mortgage specialist to have a conversation to see if a reverse mortgage would be of benefit to the senior.

Financial advisors, attorneys, CPA's accountants, real estate agents, insurance agents, mediators, and fiduciaries are professions that come to mind that, together with a reverse mortgage specialist, could *work as a team for the best interest of a mutual client*—respective professionals coming together to work for and with the mutual client. I believe this model is grossly underutilized and hope it becomes more utilized, especially as reverse mortgages continue to be seen and used more as a financial planning tool.

I share some advice based on my experiences in the hope that we all work together with integrity within our respective professions, and foster respect across different professions to all do the best thing for our mutual senior client. Advice given, and actions taken by the seniors could well have consequences decades from the time actions are taken. And as we walk farther down the retirement path, we have less time to correct any mistakes or bad advice given today.

CHAPTER TWO

When a HECM Isn't the Right Choice

I hope that one thing you get out of reading my book is that I am a huge proponent of today's HECM. But a HECM may *not* be in a homeowner's best interest[2]. So, I want to offer a little bit more advice before we launch into the HECM world.

All financial products need to be sold with the highest of integrity, whether that product comes from a bank, a financial advisor, insurance agent, or a mortgage professional. Because the HECM serves the senior market, the Federal government is especially concerned that seniors aren't taken advantage of. And we can all complain about Uncle Sam having their nose in things, but, overall, their oversight of the HECM is a good thing.

Integrity, in part, means offering the best product, structured in the best way, that best serves the client. There are situations and circumstances where a HECM is *not* the best product to offer a client. And while my following advice is not at all inclusive of all situations, I want to offer a few scenarios where a reverse mortgage may not be a good option.

First may be the homeowners may not be planning to live in their home for a long period of time. Albeit, "long time" is relative, but generally speaking at least 3 to 5 years should be the plan at the time a reverse mortgage is taken out. Reverse mortgages have costs associated with them. And if you only planned on living in your home for a year or two, the cost associated with obtaining a reverse

---

[2] CFPB Report to Congress on reverse mortgages. June 2012 / 2.7

mortgage is very high. This is an example where a person should seek out alternatives other than obtaining a reverse mortgage.

When looking into choosing a reverse mortgage, the senior homeowners really need to look at their budget, especially in the event of the loss of a spouse. The second reason obtaining a reverse mortgage may *not* be in the consumers' best interest is because if they obtain the reverse mortgage, it may not satisfy their financial needs. Instead, they may be better off selling the home and downsizing. Additionally, it may be in the seniors' best interest to consider applying for federal, state, or local programs that may provide financial assistance to seniors.

A third possibility of when a reverse mortgage may *not* be in the homeowner's best interest is if the senior wants to protect their legacy. I love a saying I recently heard regarding legacies: "Are you going to leave a legacy, live a legacy, or both?" And I believe this is an area that frequently needs additional discussion. Too often the parents want to leave their home to their children, and the children almost immediately put the house on the market to sell when the parents are, for whatever reason, no longer living in their home. While the baby boomers are redefining this, many people still want to leave their home as their legacy. And given that the reverse mortgage loan balance *increases* over time, coupled with a potential market downturn, the equity in the home could be gone. Not right nor wrong but deserving of a conversation when considering a reverse mortgage.

The fourth, and final, scenario I want to share with you why a person may *not* want to consider a reverse mortgage is because they simply do not understand it. Again, reverse mortgages are a unique mortgage instrument. Many of its features are counter-intuitive to a traditional forward mortgage. And because of this, some people simply cannot understand this product. It is for that one reason alone that they should not consider a reverse mortgage.

With my advice shared, time to learn more.

PART TWO

The Basics

CHAPTER THREE

In the Beginning

Home Equity Conversion Mortgage (HECM, pronounced *heck'em*) is the official name given by HUD (Department of Housing and Urban Development), which is the federal governmental agency that oversees the program for a mortgage more commonly known as reverse mortgage. HUD then charges the Federal Housing Administration (FHA) to oversee, operate the loan program, and provide the insurance for the product. However, it is worth noting that while FHA reverse mortgages constitute the clear majority of reverse mortgages, there are other reverse mortgage programs out there. For example, there are private reverse mortgages and jumbo reverse mortgages. Jumbo reverse mortgages would be for homes valued greater than $679,650[3]. Because the other reverse mortgage programs make up such a small percentage of the overall reverse mortgages made each year, I am only going to focus on **HUD/FHA HECM** loans.

Reverse mortgages have been around longer than most people think… in fact, a lot longer. 1961 was the year of the first reverse mortgage, and it was a savings and loan (remember those?) in Portland, Maine that made that loan[4]. Officially, it was in 1987 that Senator William Proxmire sponsored the Housing and Community Development Act of 1987 which created an FHA insurance program and a demonstration project for a Home Equity Conversion Loan. President Reagan signed the bill into law in February 1988. Today's HECM was officially born.

---

[3] HECM FHA Maximum Claim Amount effective 1.1.18

[4] CFPB Report to Congress on reverse mortgages June 2012

From 1988 until 2009, little change was made in the reverse mortgage program. Effective January 1, 2009, the HECM world opened to purchase transactions. Prior to this, they could only be used for refinances; the borrower already owned their home and had substantial equity to utilize a reverse mortgage. But now, you could purchase a home using a reverse mortgage. I cover purchasing a home with a reverse mortgage in depth in Chapter 20.

Then the economic recession that began in 2008 caused HUD to re-evaluate the HECM program. This turned into a wave of changes in the program beginning in 2013. In 2015, another major change hit the HECM world. They now require a financial assessment of the borrower(s). "Financial assessment" is a fancy term for underwriting. Prior to financial assessments, about the only condition for obtaining a reverse mortgage was having enough equity in your home to qualify. But now a senior homeowner had to qualify with both sufficient income or "capacity" and credit or "willingness". Finally, as recent as October 2, 2017, additional changes were made to the HECM program. Please know and understand now that *HECM underwriting guidelines are NOT the same as a traditional forward mortgage*.

HECM underwriting is more lenient, and if there are issues and/or shortcomings in a borrower's capacity or willingness, there may still be a couple ways to make the HECM work.

First, the HECM allows for "compensating factors". Say the death of a spouse with their associated medical bills cause issues with their credit. This is an "event" that can be "verified and documented".

The other feature of a HECM is the LESA feature (see Chapter 22) that *may* be used to still allow the borrowers to obtain their reverse mortgage. I say *may* because LESAs have allowed many borrowers to obtain a HECM they otherwise wouldn't have qualified for, but LESAs don't guarantee a loan's approval.

In addition to capacity and willingness, the property is underwritten as well. Keep in mind, it is the Federal government overseeing and insuring this loan. The Federal government sees seniors as a protected class of citizens. And they want to ensure they are living in homes that do not have health and safety issues. An appraisal is done, not only to determine the value of the home, but also to make sure there are no health and safety issues in or around the home.

Unofficially, reverse mortgages are over 50 years old. Officially, they are 30 years old this year. They have a past that rightly caused the myths and misconceptions of today. It is a complex loan, and it wasn't the best loan for most of its history. But I also have come to believe that the human nature of people will make up stories and beliefs through misunderstandings of issues. Because of this, some of the myths and misconceptions also reside in this domain. And I say this without judgment, as this is going to happen anytime we are introduced to something new in life. And reverse mortgages have a relatively long history. However, because of their recent major changes, they can be viewed as a relatively new mortgage product. They weren't the best loan out there, but between 2012 and 2017 vast changes occurred and today I believe they are great loans for the right people.

CHAPTER FOUR

Myths & Misconceptions

"Myths and misconceptions"… sounds more like a King Arthur movie of folklore and myths. But as it is with anything that has undergone a lot of change over time, and in the beginning had features that financially hurt people, it created a foundation for myths and misconceptions to be born and grow. Thankfully, with the changes that have been made to the program over the last several years, today those myths are just that: myths and misconceptions, not truths about the program.

I feel it's important to "clear the air" before even beginning to understand today's reverse mortgage. If I tried to explain the features and how reverse mortgages work while you were stuck in the belief system of one or more of these myths and misconceptions, you wouldn't "hear" what I was saying. You likely would be comparing or arguing against what I was saying compared to the myth or misconception you were holding on to.

Okay, time to clear the air.

Myth: I can lose my home. FALSE. The truth is you cannot lose your home. You can live in your home until you are 120 years old, as long as you don't "trip" a maturity event. Maturity events are the following:

a) It is your primary residence. For a married couple, only one spouse must remain in the home. This is particularly important to know in case one spouse has to go into assisted living or passes away.

b) You maintain the home. Basically, meaning keeping your home in good repair.

c) You pay real estate taxes, homeowners insurance, flood insurance, and assessment fees, as applicable.

Those points made, you cannot lose your home. You do have a lien on your home, just like you would with a traditional forward mortgage. In the event you sell the home, whether you decide to sell, a person dies, or it is no longer your primary residence, you trip a maturity event, there is a lien on the property, and it must be paid off.

A special feature of a reverse mortgage is called a *non-recourse feature.* GET THIS… THIS IS POTENTIALLY A HUGE DEAL. In the event the home is sold or foreclosed on and the balance of the loan exceeds the value of the property, "the lender can look only to the property to satisfy the loan," as opposed to holding the borrower personally liable for the debt. This repayment standard also applies to the borrower's heirs or estate when the property is sold to repay the outstanding loan."[5] This is known as a non-recourse feature. (See Chapter 13 for more on non-recourse.)

Myth: The bank owns or will own my home. FALSE. The lender has a first lien mortgage on your property, just like a lender would if you have a traditional forward mortgage on your home. But it is a lien: they do not, nor will they, own your property.

Myth: Reverse mortgages are too expensive. FALSE. Reverse mortgages, as all mortgages do, have costs associated with obtaining them. A reverse mortgage *may* have an origination fee in addition to the normal fees associated with obtaining the loan. If it has an origination fee, know the amount of an origination fee is capped by

---

[5] HECM Protocol 5.D.6.a

HUD and cannot be exceeded. Knowing there are costs associated with getting one, they *may* be expensive. If a borrower is only planning on having the loan for 2-3 years, seeking alternative financing would be recommended, as the costs associated with obtaining the reverse mortgage analyzed over a very short term would make it an expensive loan. However, obtaining a reverse mortgage and having it for potentially decades, given we are living longer, makes the cost of the reverse mortgage less with each passing year.

Myth: It sounds too good to be true. FALSE. Simply, there is no free lunch. Sounding too good to be true is most often associated with the fact that you don't have to make a principal and interest payment. The "no free lunch" part is that interest is calculated monthly, as is the mortgage insurance, and are added to your loan balance. Most people who have this belief initially "hear" the part of not making payments. When they understand that interest and mortgage insurance accrue monthly, they understand why their myth of sounding too good to be true is now truly a myth.

Myth: My children will be responsible for the debt on the home. TRUE & FALSE. A HECM is a first lien on your home. If you sell the home or it is foreclosed on, the lien needs to be paid off. So **TRUE**, if this occurs and there is equity in the home. If the home is now in an estate when this occurs, then the children would be responsible (assuming they are acting as executors for and/or heirs of the estate) to pay the existing lien at time of sale or foreclosure. However, any remaining equity goes to the homeowner/estate/heirs. **FALSE** if the loan balance exceeds the value of the home at the time of sale or foreclosure. This is when the non-recourse feature "kicks in" and covers the deficit. Subsequently, no liability would pass on to the estate or heirs.

Myth: Homeowners will have to leave their home if they run out of money. FALSE, if running out of money doesn't cause a "maturity event," which should never occur with today's financial assessment rule. But I need to go deeper with this myth.

- If a person is receiving a term or tenure payment from their reverse mortgage (more likely to happen with a tenure payment as tenure payments are for the life of the borrower), that payment will continue *regardless* of the value of their home.
- If a person has a line of credit on their reverse mortgage, the value of the line of credit will grow monthly, *regardless* of the value of their home. Subsequently, the unused portion of the value of the line of credit is always available to the homeowner.
- If a person has opted for a modified term or a modified tenure option, which combines a monthly payment with a line of credit, as I have just previously stated, the monthly payments will continue for the term or life of the borrower. The unused portion of the line of credit will always be available, *regardless* of the value of their home.

My hope is that I have cleared up most of people's myths and misconceptions by covering these most popular ones. Any further outstanding myths and misconceptions… keep reading (and I know you will) for more new information and education to dispel any remaining myths and misconceptions that you may have.

CHAPTER FIVE

How HECMs Work

First, allow me to do a little comparison with a traditional forward mortgage to help you understand how a reverse mortgage works.

First, whether a forward or a reverse mortgage, they are both mortgages. They both have liens against your property. They both must be paid off in the event you sell your home. They both charge interest: the traditional forward mortgage you pay monthly, the reverse mortgage interest accrues monthly, you have the option to make a mortgage payment, and doesn't have to be paid until a future time.

Beyond these comparisons between a traditional forward and a reverse mortgage, let's go a little deeper in the inner workings of a HECM mortgage.

A HECM is a *mortgage loan* against the borrower's primary residence that provides for cash advances to the borrower and *requires no repayment* until a future date.

The unique aspect of a reverse mortgage is that the interest payments on the loan are deferred until the end of the life of the loan. A critical distinction that many people don't know is that you *may make interest or principal and interest payments on a HECM loan.* Interest is **not** paid up-front, out-of-pocket, or monthly. This is truly unique to the reverse mortgage, as all traditional forward mortgages require a monthly principal and interest payment.

Keep in mind, there is "no free lunch," as the interest on a reverse mortgage accrues daily and is added to your loan balance monthly. Additionally, the annual mortgage insurance is added to your loan balance monthly. Borrowers get a monthly statement, so you can always see where the loan balance is.

The following features are what makes the HECM such a great loan. It isn't like a traditional forward mortgage where you look for the lowest interest rate, know it is a 30-year fixed-rate (most often) mortgage, and work to close the loan. Rather, given the features of a reverse mortgage, combined with sufficient equity, now the conversation becomes "What is best for the senior homeowner? How can a HECM be structured such that the needs and/or goals of the borrower best be met?" Therefore, countries around the world[6] are studying our HECM loan to emulate it... because it works so well!

Before I share the different ways to obtain cash, let me first explain how a mandatory obligation fits in here. If a borrower has a mandatory obligation (an existing mortgage is by far the most common mandatory obligation), that must be satisfied (paid off) first before any other options can be used. A HECM can only be in first lien position, so any existing mortgage(s) must be paid first from the HECM proceeds.

Having satisfied the existing mortgage and there is enough remaining equity, or if there is no existing mortgage, then these other features of the reverse mortgage become available to the borrower:

- **Tenure Income:** A monthly income for life
- **Term Income:** A monthly income for a set term or number of years

---

[6] Reverse Mortgage Magazine January-February 2016

- **Line of Credit:** A line of credit that contractually grows in value monthly
- **Modified Tenure:** A combination of a monthly payment for life (tenure) combined with a line of credit
- **Modified Term:** A combination of a monthly payment for a set number of years (term) and a line of credit
- **Cash-Out:** A lump sum cash distribution

Understanding better how a reverse mortgage works allows for a new conversation. Now the conversation becomes "How can I *best use* a HECM to fulfill my needs and goals?"

CHAPTER SIX

How Much Money Do I Get?

It depends. I sound like a politician with that answer. In truth, it does depend on a couple factors to determine how much of the equity in your home you are eligible to receive or have available to you.

Today it is quite easy to determine, at least close, how much money you are eligible to receive because there are a lot of websites out there with the "Principal Limit" calculator on them readily available. Think of **Principal Limit** as your maximum loan amount. It is the maximum amount of your home equity you qualify to "tap into".

While many people know to go to websites and obtain their Principal Limit, as do many mortgage professionals, very few people know how the Principal Limit is calculated.

A principal limit is a percentage of the value of the home or the maximum claim amount (currently $679,650[7]), the *lesser of the two.* The percentage used to determine the principal limit is known as the **Principal Limit Factor (PLF).** The PLF is comprised of two factors. The first factor is the age of the youngest borrower. For a married couple, this is the age of the youngest spouse. Obviously, for a single person the PLF is based on their age. HUD has created this table to cover ages 18 to 99, although past the age of 97 the amount of your home equity you can tap into does not increase, as that percentage is capped at age 97.

The second factor is based on what is called an expected rate (*see glossary for definition*). The charts for the

---

[7] Maximum Claim Amount as of January 1, 2018

expected rates are between 3% and 18%. Combining the age of the youngest borrower with the expected interest rate on the PLF table gives you a factor. Said differently, based on the age of the youngest borrower and the expected rate, HUD gives you a chart to show you the percentage of your home equity you are eligible to receive.

Once you have the PLF, which is expressed as a percentage, you simply multiply the PLF by the *lesser of* the appraised value of the home or $679,650. Where did I come up with the $679,650 figure? That is FHA's current "maximum claim amount," as FHA calls it. It could also be referred to as a maximum value of the home that the PLF can be applied to. For example, if the home was appraised at $700,000, the PLF would be based on the $679,650 because, again, that is the maximum claim amount. FHA's lending limit changes periodically and the $679,650 is the limit in effect as of January 1, 2018.

Now that you understand the PLF and how much of your home equity you can receive, you may not be eligible to receive all of your proceeds at your closing. Remember, I said between 2012 and 2017 a lot of changes occurred to the HECM program. This is one of those big changes, and I believe it's for the good of all. On June 18, 2014, HUD announced that, with certain exceptions that I will cover in a minute, HUD is limiting the initial disbursements to 60% of the principal limit. They called it the Reverse Mortgage Stabilization Act of 2013.

I wondered why they did that. Well, it turns out that the reverse mortgage industry had a practice of requiring large initial withdraws on reverse mortgages. Remember, reverse mortgages are insured loans. They are insured by the FHA Mutual Mortgage Insurance Fund (MMIF). The large draws

HUD is talking about can be said as, "Pull all my money out when I take out the loan." Simply stated, if all the funds are taken out and interest is accruing monthly, long term, the risk of owing more than the value of the home (known as being *upside down*) goes up substantially. Once a loan goes upside down, also called *negative amortization* because reverse mortgages are non-recourse loans, the insurance now must cover the deficit of the loan. HUD was beginning to see in its forecasts that the insurance fund was going to be in trouble (short of funds) if something wasn't done. Therefore, they limited the initial withdrawal of funds to 60% of the PLF unless you have a mandatory obligation. This is the exception I was referencing in the last paragraph.

Generally speaking, a mandatory obligation is a first mortgage, the upfront or initial mortgage insurance premium, any loan origination fees, closing costs, and any delinquent Federal debt. I had a client who had to satisfy a divorce decree (he had no mortgage on his home) and that, too, is considered a mandatory obligation. I want to emphasize my definition of mandatory obligations is purposely general in nature. Please consult a reverse mortgage professional for additional details.

One remaining question I haven't answered is "Can a borrower get 100% of their principal limit?" Absolutely, if the mandatory obligation is high enough. A great example of this is using a reverse mortgage to purchase a home. You would generally want to take all the money available to you (full principal limit) from the reverse mortgage to purchase your home.

Now you can begin to understand why I titled this chapter "How Much Money do I Get?" and why my initial answer was, "it depends". There are several factors that go into determining how much equity a person is eligible to receive, when they can receive it, and these factors must be coupled with how they want to receive their proceeds to meet their needs and goals.

CHAPTER SEVEN

What Can I Do with My Money?

Whatever you want. End of chapter.

Okay, maybe that is a little too high level. When you obtain funds from a HECM, it is yours to do with what you want. First, it is a loan, so it is tax free money. And it does not affect Social Security or Medicare. A reminder here. I am not a tax planner nor a financial advisor, so seek appropriate legal and or professional advice as applicable. But let me give general guidelines.

I once had a financial planner get upset with me because she thought, with all the options potentially available in how to receive funds from a reverse mortgage, I was giving investment advice. She couldn't hear that it is a loan with many options in *how* to receive the proceeds of the loan. Obviously gross miscommunication between us but that aside, reverse mortgage professionals do not and cannot give investment advice, period.

That said, let me attempt to simplify this issue. A HECM converts the equity in a home into available cash. How and when you receive the cash is (inside of the rules of the HECM) up to you. As I have covered but it is worth repeating, HECM proceeds can be accessed in one or more of the following ways:

- Pay off an existing mortgage (this is a must if an existing mortgage exists)
- Obtain a lump sum distribution of cash
- Establish a line of credit – future availability of cash
- Tenure monthly income – a monthly income for life

- Term monthly income – a monthly income for a fixed number of years
- Modified tenure is a combination of a line of credit and tenure monthly income.
- Modified term is a combination of a line of credit and term monthly income.

The flexibility of the HECM gets better[8]. As the borrower will be able to change the type of payment plan throughout the life of the loan. They may change the term of payments, receive an unscheduled payment, suspend payments, establish or terminate a line of credit, or receive the entire net principal limit in a lump sum payment[9]... all of this is based on there being enough equity to do so.

This is worth repeating. The proceeds from a HECM is not taxable income. It is a loan against your primary residence. However, if the funds are placed in an investment account that earns interest, that interest is likely taxable.

You also may be able to deduct the mortgage interest paid on a HECM loan should you decide to pay down the balance of the HECM. Then the interest paid is mortgage interest, and as such would be treated like paying mortgage interest on a traditional forward mortgage. Also, it is worth noting that fees associated with obtaining a reverse mortgage may be tax deductible.

With the understanding that there are many ways to possibly obtain the proceeds from a reverse mortgage and they are tax-free dollars, what could you do with the money? Here are some ideas for you to ponder:

---

[8] Most of these options are NOT available on the Fixed Rate HECM

[9] HUD Handbook 4235.1 REV-1, 1-6

- Pay off an existing first mortgage. Reduces monthly expenses, increases monthly cash flow.
- Remodel your home to accommodate aging limitations, allowing the homeowner(s) to stay in their home.
- Maintain a line of credit (that grows monthly) for health emergencies and life's surprises.
- Cover monthly expenses to be able to hold onto other assets, allowing them to grow in value.
- Salary replacement.
- Pay for health insurance until Medicare eligible.
- Pay for Medicare Supplement Insurance.
- Combine life tenure payments with Social Security and income generated by assets to replace salary.
- Pay children's or grandchildren's college or professional education.
- Ability to tap into a line of credit for cash to get through the ups and downs of investment cycles.
- Buy a new home.
- Buy a second home.
- Use the proceeds from a reverse mortgage for the down payment of investment property with the investment property supplementing retirement income.
- Pay for long-term care insurance.
- Fill the income gap in retirement income caused by lower than expected return on investments.
- Pay for short-term in-home care or physical therapy following an accident or medical procedure.
- Estate planning and/or preservation
- Convert a room or a basement into a living facility for an aging parent, relative, or caregiver.

- Longevity insurance. Proceeds available to help insure income through retirement years.
- Pay real estate taxes, homeowners insurance, and other costs associated with homeownership.
- Delay collecting Social Security until age 70 when your monthly benefit stops increasing.
- Pay off credit cards, student loans, or other debt.
- Cover monthly expenses between jobs or during a career transition without having to tap into savings.
- If assistance for daily living was needed but moving to a full-time assisted living facility wasn't necessary, proceeds from a HECM could be used to pay for part-time in-home care.
- Cover expenses including possible income and capital gains tax consequences from selling assets.
- Purchase health related technology, allowing the homeowner to stay in their home.
- Work interruption income.
- Gifting for estate planning purposes.
- Proceeds to settle a divorce.
- Have FUN! Use the proceeds to check off items on your bucket list. Spend responsibly.

CHAPTER EIGHT

Reverse Mortgage Line of Credit

Today's HECMs have the feature of a Line of Credit, HECM LOC (given the borrower has the equity to qualify for one). This single feature is a primary reason to utilize a reverse mortgage as a retirement planning tool. But before I share more about it, allow me to clear up some misconceptions surrounding it.

When I say a reverse mortgage has a line of credit feature, most people's definition of a line of credit is what they know about a traditional forward mortgage Home Equity Line of Credit (HELOC). These loans were very popular pre-real estate market crash of 2008. And other than sharing the words "Line of Credit" and utilizing your home's equity, little else is the same between them. Let's take a look by comparing the two:

Traditional HELOC

- Uses the equity in your home as your line of credit. Maximum available funds are a percentage of the value of your home. As a simple example, a bank may give you 80% of the value of your home as the dollar amount for your line of credit. $300,000 home, 80% of $300,000 equals $240,000. This assumes no existing first mortgage.
- Principal balance must be paid back.
- They are adjustable rate mortgages, typically with a 18% lifetime interest rate cap.
- Cancelable! The lender can cancel the loan and call it due and payable.

- Usually have an initial period where the payments are interest only. For example, for the first 5 or 10 years, the borrower can pay interest only on the funds drawn on the line of credit.
- After the initial interest only draw period, the balance is going to be amortized. Said differently, the borrower has been paying interest only for, say, five years. At the end of the five years the bank is going to require principal and interest payments to be paid back. Typically, principal and interest payments are set up on a 10-year payback period, known as a 10-year term. The big potential downside of this is that the payment *will go up* and could actually double. Doubling a payment when you are more years into your retirement is not what you want to happen!

In summary, a retiree wants *less* fixed costs every month. With a traditional HELOC, not only is there a fixed cost monthly, but that fixed cost absolutely will increase when the loan amortizes, and principal and interest payments must be made.

HECM LOC

- Uses the equity in your home as your line of credit. Maximum available funds are the principal limit. This assumes no existing mortgage on the home.
- Principal balance does NOT have to be paid back. Monthly payments are optional. Well, okay, it does have to be paid, but not in monthly payments. Refer to Chapter 17 for maturity events.
- Only available with the adjustable rate HECM.

- Current lifetime interest rate cap is approximately 9.5%.
- Qualification for a HECM is less strict than a traditional forward mortgage.
- Has no term limits or balloon payments. Live to be 120, God bless. It is unlike a traditional HELOC mortgage with terms (typically) of 10 or 15 years.
- They are NON-CANCELABLE! Meaning as long as a maturity event isn't triggered, the lender can not cancel the Line of Credit.
- Here is the **BIG DEAL**. A **HECM LOC VALUE INCREASES** every month regardless of the value of the home.

Note: When I say "approximately" in my explanation of the lifetime interest rate cap and credit line growth, these figures change slightly and frequently because the rates change potentially daily based on the market.

Please understand, when I say the HECM LOC grows every month regardless of the value of the home, I mean *regardless of the value of the home.* Remember, this is a non-recourse loan and as long as it is the borrower's primary residence, the taxes and insurance bills are paid, and the home maintained, they live in their home until they are 120 years old… and every month the line of credit grows. If the property value increases or decreases, it makes no difference in the line of credit growth. This is unprecedented in the world of mortgages and why HECM LOCs are an excellent risk management tool for fluctuating real estate values, stock market volatility, and long-term care events.

The HECM LOC is an "open ended" line of credit, meaning the borrower can use it and pay it down and use it again, similar in this respect to a credit card. You charge on the credit card and pay the balance down or off. This is the definition of *open-ended*. If you chose to pay it down, you wouldn't want to pay it off, as most lenders would close the line of credit if you did. You would want to keep a minimum of $100 on the line of credit as most lenders require this as a minimum balance to keep the account open. However, a critical note that I have had some clients get confused with: when it is time to sell the home, it is only the line of credit *balance* that is paid off, not the available line of credit amount. I've had several people think the available line of credit needs to be paid off. WRONG. Think of having a $5,000 limit on your credit card and only owing $500. If you wanted to pay it down (remember, you want to leave a minimum balance), you wouldn't pay down the $5,000. You pay down the balance owed: $500. If you don't use it, you don't pay for it. I understand the confusion, as this feature is unique to reverse mortgages and takes time to understand.

A little more information on a reverse LOC. Let's use the example of a person who had a $50,000 first mortgage that was paid off with their reverse mortgage, additionally, they have a $100,000 line of credit. If they want to pay down the $50,000 mortgage balance, the amount they pay down the outstanding balance will increase the available funds on the line of credit. This is a potentially powerful tool. Say the couple is in their 60's and still working. If they make payments reducing the principal balance, and in doing so increase their line of credit, the increasing available funds in the line of credit also grows, as all lines of credit do on HECM LOCs. Now they pay down or off their $50,000, incur mortgage interest payments, i.e., mortgage interest may be a write-off on taxes and their line of credit is growing. Fast forward to when they are in their 80's or beyond and they will have substantially more funds available in their line of credit than had they left just their $100,000 to grow.

I often ask my clients, "When is the best time to borrow money?" The answer is "When you don't need it". This is why establishing a line of credit earlier than later is so important. You don't want to wait until something happens and scramble to obtain a loan. This is especially true with the HECM LOC because it is growing for you every month. And in 20-30 years that can be the difference in tens or hundreds of thousands of dollars available to the borrower. Establishing it early gives you liquidity, available cash, in the event you need it.

In summary, the HECM LOC is an excellent retirement planning tool! With a guaranteed growth rate on the line of credit, the earlier the HECM is obtained the more time it has to grow. Line of credit availability that is growing, coupled with no required monthly payments is why many financial advisors are supporting HECM LOCs.

CHAPTER NINE

Pay Off an Existing Mortgage

This is often confusing to many people I speak to. Yes, if you want to obtain a reverse mortgage you must pay off your existing first mortgage. "But how does that work?" is the question I have heard several times.

It works exactly like refinancing your existing traditional forward mortgage with a new traditional forward mortgage because you found a lower rate, which many people have done at some point in their life. You currently have an existing mortgage (called a mandatory obligation in the HECM world) and you refinance your home, and the new mortgage is now a reverse mortgage. It is that simple. Somehow, I think people hear "reverse mortgage" and they think it must be more complicated. While they are a complex mortgage, don't overcomplicate this issue.

I must mention refinancing to reduce an interest rate. That is what we are taught. Get a mortgage, get the lowest rate. Rates go down, refinance again and get a lower rate. We are always chasing the lowest interest rate. And that is a great thing... in the traditional forward mortgage world, not in the reverse mortgage world.

In the reverse mortgage world, you don't shop for the lowest rate like a traditional forward mortgage. Albeit, it is great, everyone wants the lowest possible rate, but this is not the primary reason people get a reverse mortgage. In fact, obtaining the lowest possible rate may *not* be in your best interest!

People get reverse mortgages for *peace of mind and quality of life*. And often paying off an existing mortgage obtains both objectives. No longer having a principal and interest payment and possibly having the real estate taxes and homeowner's insurance covered as well gives people peace of mind that they don't have to pay their "mortgage payment" ever again. And it fulfills the second objective: quality of life. At the least, not having a principal and interest payment adds to a person's or couple's monthly cash flow, and additional cash flow gives a better quality of life.

For some people, not having a mortgage payment means the difference between paying the mortgage or buying groceries or having their prescriptions filled. Not having a mortgage payment (Principal & Interest) *increases their monthly cash flow* because they don't have the expense of their principal and interest payment. I have experienced clients who found that a substantial amount of their household income was gone due to the death of a spouse. And the surviving spouse was in a world of hurt having to still pay a mortgage but now with only one income instead of the three they had.

Going full circle, yes you can pay off an existing mortgage utilizing a reverse mortgage. But let's give more understanding to this issue, as the potential of many more options lie ahead. There may be only enough funds available in a reverse mortgage to pay off the existing first mortgage. But let's assume there is more funds available in a borrower's HECM than needed to pay off the existing first mortgage... then what?

Options! This is where a reverse mortgage comes alive and serves the senior homeowner in ways *they* choose. I covered this in Chapter 7, but let's briefly cover this again, as many senior borrowers can utilize these options. For the sake of example, let's assume a small mortgage was paid off and there is, say, $150,000 still available in the reverse mortgage. The following are the options available to the borrower:

- Take a lump sum of cash.
- Tenure payments. Establish a monthly income for the rest of your life.
- Term payments. Establish a fixed monthly income for a set term (fixed number of years).
- Establish a line of credit.
- Modified tenure payments: a combination of a line of credit and tenure payments.
- Modified term payments: a combination of a line of credit and term payments.

Given enough equity you can pay off an existing mortgage, get a small amount of cash and take the balance of your equity and get a modified tenure payment. WOW!

Also, worth noting is a HECM needs to be structured to meet your needs and goals today. But we all know and have experienced life show up despite our best plans. If life shows up different tomorrow, know that you can modify your HECM, given enough equity, to meet your needs and goals of tomorrow. One example of this is upon the death of a spouse, and the loss of their income, a line of credit may be converted into monthly payments. This would give additional monthly income to supplement (or replace) the deceased spouses income.

HECMs can only be in first position and you cannot obtain a second mortgage (line of credit, for example). But given enough equity, paying off the existing first mortgage borrowers may still have many options available to them and use a reverse mortgage to insure their peace of mind and quality of life through their retirement years... no matter how many years that ends up being.

CHAPTER TEN

What to Consider Before I Proceed

A reverse mortgage as a retirement planning tool, instead of a loan of last resort, begs a few questions and some considerations before you jump into the deep end with this loan[10]. There are currently over one million HECMs having been sold since their inception. With the overhaul of them in the last several years, they are a proven versatile financial tool. Let's look at key questions you need to ask yourself, or as a couple you need to discuss, before proceeding with any loan application.

Let's consider a question that on the surface seems simple, but I have seen too many seniors who haven't taken this first question seriously and because of that face financial hardship. Question number one: *How do you intend to use your reverse mortgage proceeds?*

The blessing and potential curse of a reverse mortgage is its flexibility. Your home equity, simply stated, is turned into cash and what do you want to do with it? The answer is, outside of paying off an existing first mortgage to get your HECM, whatever you want to do with the proceeds. Eligible homeowners have gotten reverse mortgages for many reasons, including:

- Repairing or modifying their home to meet the physical needs of getting older
- Supplementing retirement income to meet expenses
- Managing the costs of in-home care
- Paying off an existing mortgage

---

[10] National Reverse Lenders Association booklet, Reverse Mortgage Self-Evaluation: A Checklist of Key Considerations.

- Paying bills
- Paying property taxes and/or homeowners insurance
- Delaying Social Security
- Providing a source of funds for living expenses in lieu of liquidating financial investments during a times of market downturn or disruption
- Establishing a line of credit for use as a financial safety net
- Helping retirement savings last longer
- Purchasing a home

A good plan is priceless and can help to eliminate financial hardship or crisis in your future. I invite you to look at this question beyond any immediate needs you may have, looking both short and long term.

The second question fits right in with the reason I wrote this book: education. While you are beginning to have a new perspective on reverse mortgages and understand them better, the second question goes deeper in understanding a reverse mortgage after you close. The question now is *do you fully understand your obligations as a borrower under a reverse mortgage loan?*

Too often the goal with HECMs is shortsighted. For example, a borrower is thinking about not having a mortgage payment and that becomes the beginning and end of the story. That's great, no mortgage payments, but a HECM is a collateral loan. Which means the lender has a vested interest in the safety and condition of the property. As such, there are conditions to be met for as long as you have a reverse mortgage.

First, the home must be your primary residence. Sure, go travel, enjoy life, take a world tour and be gone several months. But at the end of the day, is this home secured by a HECM your primary residence? Additionally, you must pay the real estate taxes, homeowners insurance, any association fees, and maintain the home. This is common sense stuff, simple and not unreasonable, yet they are things you are committing to when you take out a reverse mortgage and you need to know what you are committing to.

Moving right along to our next key consideration. *If you are married, will your spouse be a co-borrower on the loan?* Remember, borrowers of HECM need to be 62 years old or older. If your spouse is not 62, there are special rules, and I have devoted Chapter 12 to covering that issue. If your spouse is 62 or older, the question still needs to be asked: are they going to be on the loan? Spouses have to meet the same requirements as the borrower. If a spouse isn't 62 or they don't want to be on the loan, speak with your reverse mortgage professional to understand your options.

How will your reverse mortgage be repaid? Hold on, you are thinking you don't have to make payments! And this is where many people have the reaction of "this is too good to be true." And it would seem too good to be true if you didn't have to pay back the loan. The critical distinction here is you *don't have to make payments, but the loan has to be repaid.* (Refer to Chapters 17 and 19 for more details on paying or having to repay the loan.)

A reverse mortgage becomes due when the last surviving borrower or remaining eligible non-borrowing spouse passes away, permanently vacates or sells the home, or if one of the maturity events are triggered. As is said, "No one wants to die, but everyone wants to go to heaven," the fact is we are all going to die. Planning how the loan is going to be repaid when a reverse mortgage is obtained is an important consideration to address.

A reverse mortgage is a mortgage, a lien on the property, and just like a traditional forward mortgage, when the home is sold the existing mortgage is paid first from the sale proceeds. Whether there is no equity or a lot of equity, advance planning for how the loan is going to be paid in the future is good financial sense.

A reverse mortgage is a loan, but the next consideration before you take out a HECM relates to *do you receive assistance under any government programs that are based on your current income?* As a loan, reverse mortgages do NOT affect regular Social Security or Medicare benefits. However, in the case of programs that are "means-tested" benefits or public assistance programs, a reverse mortgage may affect your eligibility. If you are receiving or thinking about applying for a government program, check into this issue before you apply for a reverse mortgage.

None of us know if we are going to be here to have dinner tonight. But the next question needs to be addressed: *How long do you and your spouse plan on living in your home?* The reason for this question is because, like virtually all mortgages, there is a cost associated with obtaining them. If you are thinking of staying in your home for a relatively short period of time, you may want to consider alternatives to a reverse mortgage. If you took out a reverse mortgage today and sold your home within a year, it quite likely became a very expensive loan. As with any financial product, the longer you can amortize the cost of obtaining them, the less expensive they become.

One last question for you: *Have you considered other strategies to supplement your retirement income?* There are many programs potentially available such as housing assistance, tax deferral programs, home repair grants, food stamps, fuel assistance, social services, and, if one's health permits, working a part-time job. I recently read an article about how much seniors have to offer and the "new trend" is for them to be consultants and get paid for consulting/coaching others in what they know best. Often this is what they have spent their entire career doing and they love doing it.

The baby boomers aren't doing retirement like previous generations. In fact, they have cut a new path through life from any other previous generation. I believe this question especially calls for creativity and thinking outside the box. Hell… throw the box away. How creative can you be to generate additional income if you need or want to?

I invite you to spend some time on these questions. The answers aren't etched in stone. You can edit or recreate your plan, but without a plan too often one's life becomes like a ship in the sea without a rudder.

CHAPTER ELEVEN

Counseling

The decision to get a reverse mortgage is an important one. Given the changes that have occurred to the program, it has never been more important to understand a reverse mortgage and what it can do for the senior homeowner. The Department of Housing and Urban Development (HUD) and the Federal Housing Administration (FHA) want to ensure that you make an informed decision and that a HECM will meet your needs. Said differently, HUD and FHA want to make sure a reverse mortgage is a good fit for the borrower and the borrower knows what type of loan they are obtaining.

Subsequently, before a person can apply for a reverse mortgage, HUD requires them to attend a counseling session[11]. All HUD counseling agencies are an independent third party to the transaction. It doesn't matter which counseling agency a person chooses, they are all "reading from the same book." And it isn't just the borrower(s) who must have counseling. It is *all* borrowers: borrower, co-borrower, non-borrowing spouse, guardians, conservators, and/or Power of Attorneys. In short, everyone involved in the transaction must complete counseling[12].

However, heirs are not required to attend counseling, but they are encouraged to attend. I am glad this is encouraged, as there are several benefits to an heir attending counseling. In an example of elderly parents, having at least one child

---

[11] Housing Counseling Handbook 7610.0, HECM Counseling Protocol, Chapter 4

[12] HUD doesn't require but rather recommends a non-borrowing spouse attend counseling. However, many lenders will require a non-borrowing spouse to attend counseling.

attend counseling with them enables the child to help Mom and Dad better understand the reverse mortgage. Another benefit of the child attending the counseling is that if the parents have questions in the future, the child is better able to answer their questions. Interesting how we never outgrow Mom and Dad. The "child" I am referring to here could be in their 60's, yet still the child.

Because a person must obtain counseling prior to a reverse mortgage application, this augments the reason to have an in-depth discussion with a reverse mortgage specialist *prior to attending counseling*. A reverse mortgage specialist will be able to educate you on the features of a reverse mortgage and answer questions you have. Now you are much better informed and educated when you attend your HUD counseling session. The last thing I want at a HUD counseling session are surprises. And the better educated borrowers are, the more confident they are with the decision they have made (whether or not to proceed).

HUD counseling is generally allowed to be done over the phone. You can go into a counseling center and do it person if you choose. A few states mandate it be done in person. Your reverse mortgage specialist will tell you if you have to do your counseling in person or if you have the choice of doing it in person or over the phone (this varies by state). Borrowers are provided a list of HUD-approved agencies from their reverse mortgage specialist and it is totally up to them to choose the counseling agency. It is illegal for any loan officer to "steer" a borrower to a specific counseling agency.

Once you have decided to proceed with a reverse mortgage, determined who will attend the counseling, and the appointment is set, what should you expect in your counseling session? Remember, only you can decide if a reverse mortgage is best for you, period.

The counselor's role is to educate you about the features of reverse mortgages and the appropriateness of a reverse mortgage or other financial options to meet your needs. The counselor should not tell you whether or not to proceed with a reverse mortgage, or which reverse mortgage product to use, but should provide guidance and resources to enable you to make an informed decision. The counselor must provide ongoing support to you throughout the process.

The following are the key objectives the HUD Counselor will cover with you in your counseling session. Their goal is to educate you on these objectives:

- How reverse mortgages work and the implications of reverse mortgages
- The appropriateness of a reverse mortgage for your personal and financial situation, and possible financial alternatives to reverse mortgages

The following topics must be thoroughly covered in every reverse mortgage counseling session:

- Client Needs and Circumstances
- Features of Reverse Mortgages
- Client Responsibilities Under a Reverse Mortgage
- Costs to Obtain a Reverse Mortgage
- Financial/Tax Implications of a Reverse Mortgage
- Financial or Social Service Alternatives to Reverse Mortgages

- Warnings About Potential Reverse Mortgage/Insurance Fraud Schemes and Elder Abuse

The National Council on Aging (NCOA) maintains a non-profit service called Benefits Eligibility. Your HUD Counselor may inform you of this service. Benefits Eligibility is linked to 15 different public benefit programs designed to help and support seniors to stay in their home and meet their financial obligations.

Once the counseling is complete, the counselor will email, fax, or snail mail you (your choice), your HUD Counseling Certificate. The counselor will have signed and dated it. You also have to sign and date it and then the completed HUD Counseling Certificate is given to the lender. Again, no lender can "turn on" or begin a HECM application until the counseling is completed.

Now knowing you need to obtain counseling and what is covered, I want to give you a "punch list" of items to do or to have prior to scheduling your HUD counseling session:

1. **Meet with a Reverse Mortgage Specialist** to discuss whether a reverse mortgage is the best option for you. Most forward mortgage professionals have no idea how a reverse mortgage works, let alone the intricacies of them and how to best structure a HECM. Take your time to educate and understand how a reverse mortgage works by meeting with a qualified professional.

2. **Your pre-counseling package.** The following are the documents to expect from your reverse mortgage specialist:

     a. Reverse Mortgage Comparison. This will list a minimum of three different scenarios, including an adjustable rate option and a fixed rate option.
     b. Loan Amortization Schedule
     c. Total Annual Loan Cost (TALC) rate disclosure
     d. A list of HUD Approved Counselors
     e. *"Preparing for Your Counseling Session"* document
     f. *"Use Your Home to Stay at Home"* booklet from the National Council on Aging (NCOA)

3. **Complete the counseling session** with a HUD approved counselor. The counselor will email or send the certificate to you upon completion of your counseling. Remember, the lender cannot "turn on" your HECM loan application until a fully signed and dated counseling certificate is provided to them.

4. **Application time.** By completing steps 1 through 3 on this punch list you are now educated, informed, and can feel confident in moving forward and having a HECM to fulfill your needs and goals.

At this point in your decision to go forward with a reverse mortgage, you should feel very confident in your choice and your understanding of not only the features of the product, but also how it is being structured to meet your financials needs and goals. You will have spent an hour or more with the reverse mortgage specialist educating yourself on a reverse mortgage. Additionally, the reverse mortgage specialist will be able to show you a reverse mortgage with "your numbers." At this point an estimate of your home value will have to be used, but you will be able to see the figures of a reverse mortgage specific to your age, estimated home value, and structured to meet your needs and goals.

You will have had your HUD Counseling session, which is generally about 90 minutes long. You should expect to have invested a minimum of 3 to 4 hours at this point educating yourself and understanding if and how a reverse mortgage may benefit you. We are talking about your financial future and, in my strong bias, this is extremely important time and energy you have put into making the best choices for your financial future. Congrats! But you aren't done yet...

PART THREE

More Things I Need to Know

CHAPTER TWELVE

My Spouse Isn't 62

Ah, the good ol' days: you were married or not… simple. Today we have a spouse, a non-borrowing spouse, a common law spouse, an ineligible non-borrowing spouse, and an eligible non-borrowing spouse. Wow, that is confusing! Well, allow me to un-confuse this issue and make sense out of it.

Remember, you must be 62 to obtain a reverse mortgage. All good when both spouses are 62 or older. We proceed with the reverse mortgage, and the principal limit (maximum loan amount) is based on the age of the youngest spouse.

But what happens when one spouse is NOT 62? The pre-62-year-old spouse is now referred to as a non-borrowing spouse. The definition of a non-borrowing spouse includes common law spouses. In fact, a non-borrowing spouse, defined by HUD, is "the spouse, as determined by the law of the state in which the spouse and mortgagor reside or the state of the celebration, of the HECM mortgagor *at the time of closing* (my italics added) and who also is not a mortgagor".[13] Notice, the definition is "at time of closing." Here is an example worth noting. A single senior obtains a reverse mortgage today. A few years later they find puppy love and marries. The new spouse is NOT a non-borrowing spouse! The new spouse was not a spouse at the time of closing of the reverse mortgage.

This basically means three things. One, the principal limit factor will be based on the non-borrowing spouse's age.

---

[13] HUD Mortgagee Letters 2014-07 & 2015-02

Two, the non-borrowing spouse will not be on the mortgage, and three, the non-borrowing spouse will remain on title to the home. I am betting you are thinking this isn't sounding so good?

Well, it wasn't so good historically because non-borrowing spouses were not protected if their spouse died. However, as of August 14, 2014, HUD[14] stepped in, with the encouragement of AARP, and made changes to the reverse mortgage to protect the spouses who weren't 62. Actually, not being 62 is only one reason for being a non-borrowing spouse. There are additional reasons for a spouse to be a non-borrowing spouse.

Here are some good examples of a spouse being a non-borrowing spouse. Many seniors have been married at least once before and often their children are from a previous marriage, so for estate planning purposes they may want their children to inherit their estates. Subsequently, they may not want their current spouse to be on the loan or title to the home. Also, there are couples with pre-nuptial agreements and couples who don't plan on staying married. Again, examples of the benefits the non-borrowing spouse affords some couples.

Let me take you back to the beginning of this issue. Prior to August 14, 2014, if the spouse died the surviving non-borrowing spouse had basically no rights to the home. The non-borrowing spouse wasn't on the loan and wasn't on the title (doesn't own the home). The borrower dies, and the surviving non-borrowing spouse is faced with a loan that is "due and payable." Well, they could refinance the home and pay off the existing reverse mortgage… assuming there

---

[14] HUD Mortgage Letter 2014-07

was equity in the home and the surviving spouse qualified for a new loan. Historically, too often there wasn't, and they didn't. This certainly gave reverse mortgages bad press!

With the changes HUD made in the HECM program effective August 14, 2014, HUD decided to give non-borrowing spouses additional rights. First, the loan is now NOT due and payable upon the death of the borrower. Now, the loan is not due and payable until the non-borrowing spouse dies, or a maturity event is triggered. This time period between the death of the borrower and when the non-borrowing spouse dies or moves out of the home is called the "Deferral Period."

Let's look at what happens during this Deferral Period. If there was a tenure or term payments being made, they stop. If there was a line of credit, no additional withdraws can be made on it. No cash withdraw can be made. What happens is the mortgage balance continues to accrue interest and the annual mortgage insurance premium continues to be charged to the HECM monthly. The non-borrowing spouse, remember, is on title (owns the home) and can live there for the rest of their life or until a maturity event is tripped.

For the Deferral Period to apply the following conditions must be met:

- The non-borrowing spouse must have been the spouse at the time of the loan closing and have remained the spouse for the duration of the HECM mortgagor's lifetime.
- The non-borrowing spouse must have been properly disclosed to the mortgagee at the origination of the

HECM and named as non-borrowing spouse in the HECM loan documents.

- The non-borrowing spouse must have occupied and continue to occupy the property securing the HECM as their principal residence.

Everything I have discussed so far is for an ELIGIBLE non-borrowing spouse. With this new law that HUD implemented in 2014, some lenders argued that some spouses were not "qualified" and as such their age shouldn't be used to determine the borrower's Principal Limit. In 2015, HUD modified the non-borrower spouse definition, adding an "INELIGIBLE" non-borrowing spouse[15]. An ineligible spouse is defined as:

- Generally, does NOT occupy the home
- Does NOT have their age included in the calculation of the borrower's Principal Limit
- Is NOT protected by the non-borrowing spouse's "due and payable" deferral provisions.

There you have it, I have covered all those spousal categories I shared in the opening of the chapter. Simply stated, if both spouses are 62 years old or older, they are borrowers. And for couples who can afford to wait until both of them are 62, it may be their best option.

For couples where one of them is not yet 62, including common law marriage states like Arizona where I live, the vast majority of non-borrowing spouses are in the category of an eligible non-borrowing spouse. If I haven't covered you yet, you would be an ineligible non-borrowing spouse. Basically, of all the categories I previously listed, it comes

---

[15] HUD Mortgagee Letter 2015-02

down to three categories into which a spouse can fall.

Overall, the changes that were made in August of 2014, 2015, and now in 2017 are good for the senior homeowners, in that they protect the non-borrowing spouse. I can't imagine telling a couple who had been married and lived in their home a long time that when the borrower (chances are the husband) passed away, the wife was facing a due and payable clause. Now the non-borrowing spouse has the peace of mind and the dignity to remain in their home after the loss of their spouse.

CHAPTER THIRTEEN

Non-Recourse Provision

Non-recourse... say what? What is it? How does it work? Non-recourse provisions are used somewhat frequently in commercial loans. I had never heard of it being used in any residential loan until I entered the reverse mortgage profession.

Reverse mortgages are negative amortization loans, which means they have the *potential* for the borrower to owe more than the value of the home. They are also federally insured loans. Reverse mortgages require mortgage insurance: both "up-front" (Initial Mortgage Insurance Premium) of 2% of the *value of the home*, paid as a lump sum at closing, and then an annual fee of 0.5% paid monthly based on the loan balance. This mortgage insurance is for the benefit of the *borrower.* And one of the benefits of mortgage insurance is to ensure that if the loan balance were to exceed the value of the home, the insurance pays the deficit (negative balance or the amount "under water").

One of the concerns I have heard is that a reverse mortgage is "too good to be true." This non-recourse feature is why people often say that. But this is why FHA has the insurance fund, called the *Mutual Mortgage Insurance Fund (MMIF).* This is the insurance or pool of funds that is used to insure reverse mortgages if the loan balance exceeds the value of the home.

The non-recourse provision of a HECM loan is one of the most beneficial features of the reverse mortgage. Period. Here is a quote directly from HUD on the definition of the non-recourse provision:

"Non-recourse" means that if a lender takes legal action against the borrower for default on the loan, the lender can look only to the property to satisfy the loan, as opposed to holding the borrower personally liable for the debt. The lender can foreclose and recover as much as it can through proceeds of the foreclosure sale.[16]

This is huge! The first benefit of this is that it should give the HECM borrowers the peace of mind that they will not be leaving a debt to their children, family, or heirs. It should also give peace of mind to the children, family, or heirs that if the homeowner lives a very long time, and/or if the property value declines, FHA will pay the deficit of the loan balance. The non-recourse provision insures the children, family, or heirs won't inherit debt.

Some people mistakenly take this to mean that the borrower (or the borrower's estate) could pay off the loan balance of the HECM for the lesser of the mortgage balance or the appraised value of the property while retaining ownership of the home. This is *not* correct. Rather, the non-recourse provision simply means that if the borrower (or estate) does not/cannot pay the balance when due because the balance due on the mortgage loan is greater than the value of the home, the mortgagee's (lender) remedy is limited to foreclosure and the borrower will not be personally liable for any deficiency resulting from the foreclosure.

The borrower not being personally liable for any deficiencies also means that no matter the size of their estate, the lender can only use the home as collateral against the loan balance. The borrower could be a

---

[16] HECM Protocol Chapter 5, Section D

millionaire and the home hundreds of thousands of dollars "upside down" and the lender can only use the collateral of the home. The lender cannot go after the assets of the borrower or the borrower's estate to make up the difference between the value of the home and the balance of the loan.

The non-recourse feature is one of the primary features of the "new" reverse mortgage that makes it a great loan. In addition to the previously mentioned benefits of the non-recourse feature, think of it also with the line of credit. Remember, the line of credit grows monthly, *regardless of the value of the home.* Who do you think pays the deficit if the line of credit exceeds the value of the home? The FHA insurance pays it via the non-recourse feature!

In Chapters 7 & 10 I gave examples of what you could use a reverse mortgage for. In Chapter 8 I explained the line of credit feature. I hope you are beginning to or by now you are understanding how powerful and diverse a retirement planning tool a reverse mortgage is. Add the non-recourse feature to this equation and now I have come to the belief that everyone who qualifies for a reverse mortgage should have one, if for no other reason than to have a line of credit as "insurance" of future liquidity *that is guaranteed regardless of the value of their home in the future.*

This is all good stuff, but you need to know more…please continue.

CHAPTER FOURTEEN

What if: Sell, Move, or Die?

For the sake of example and simplicity, let's assume you close on your reverse mortgage today. Given that you now have a reverse mortgage, there are basically three ways to get out of a reverse mortgage.

One of the current trends with seniors today is they are moving back to family. Moving back to where they moved from a few years ago. I personally fall in this category, so I know well the feelings of these seniors. Since I fall in this demographic, let me use myself as an example.

I had lived in the Chicago suburbs for 20 years before my wife and I moved to Arizona in 2008. At the time we moved my kids were married but neither one had kids. So, moving to Arizona was an easy, seemingly natural move for us at the time. Fast forward nine years and both of my children and their families live relatively close to each other in the burbs of Chicago. And now I have four granddaughters! I feel the strain on the heart strings every time I get on the plane in Chicago to come back to Arizona. My example of becoming a grandparent is one of two major reasons seniors are moving back "home" or where at least one of their children live.

The other reason is the senior's health. As we age, too often the body just doesn't shut off one day… it slowly falls apart. In doing so, additional medical assistance is often needed, whether in the form of in-home health care or just someone to check on them on a regular basis. From this relatively minor care all the way to a nursing home or assisted living facility, either way, at this point in life a lot of seniors are choosing to move close to family.

The other reason I will address is when one spouse passes away, and the surviving spouse moves close to their family. I have touched on basically three different reasons a person with a reverse mortgage would want or need to sell their home. So how does this work? Can you sell your home? If so, when?

In one way, having a reverse mortgage works exactly like a traditional forward mortgage in this respect. You sell your home, you have a mortgage, and the mortgage needs to be paid off at the sale of your home. But this is where the similarity stops. With a traditional forward mortgage, you are paying principal and interest monthly so the balance decreases every month. With a reverse mortgage, the principal balances increase every month (typically, as you can make payments and/or principal reduction payment(s) on a reverse mortgage).

Remember, the assumption I began this chapter with is you closed on your reverse mortgage today. If a life event showed up tomorrow, God bless, sell your home, pay off your mortgage, put the equity in your pocket, and go do what you need to do. My point is you may sell your home at any time. There is no pre-payment penalty. There is no set term in how long you must have the mortgage. I had one client who passed away about two months after he closed on the loan. The house went up for sale.

So, we just covered point one, what if you want to sell your home. Let's move on to what if you move out of your home. And there are a few scenarios to cover here.

First, you are going to move out of your home for a few reasons, one being you wish to sell it, and I just covered that. Now I want to cover if a homeowner needs to go into an assisted living facility. They can no longer live in their home. Subsequently, it is no longer their primary residence.

If they are married and one spouse has to go into assisted living while the other spouse continues to stay in the home as their primary residence, all is good. The spouse still living in the home can stay there as long as they want unless a maturity event is triggered.

However, if it is the last surviving spouse or a single person, once a person has to move out because they can no longer live on their own, they (assuming they have the capacity to make these decisions) must sell their home within one year after vacating their home. Actually, they have six months plus two 90-day extensions (generally approved by HUD) for a total of one year to sell the home. If they don't have the capacity to make these decisions, then it would be up to someone with a Power of Attorney or a fiduciary to step in and handle the sale of the home.

The third possibility is when the borrower dies (or if a couple when the last spouse dies), then the heirs have some choices to make. The first is to ask two questions. First, is the home upside down? (Is the loan balance greater than the value of the home?) Second, does one of the heirs want to keep the home?

If an heir wants to keep the property, there are two options. First, they can purchase the home for 95% of the current appraised home value. Here is one of the great reasons for the non-recourse provision: if the home is upside down in value, the non-recourse provision "kicks in" and covers the deficit between the loan balance and the 95% of the home's appraised value... which becomes the purchase price to the heir.

If the heir wants to keep the home and the home is not upside down, they must pay off the existing mortgage balance. Generally, this means obtaining a new mortgage to pay off the existing reverse mortgage.

If the heirs don't want to keep the property, this too comes with two options. First, is there equity in the home? If not, the heirs sign a deed-in-lieu of foreclosure, relinquishing the home to the lender... end of story. Remember, non-recourse!

If there is equity in the home, the heirs sell the home and pay off the reverse mortgage. The proceeds (or net equity) from the sale of the home is then passed onto the heirs or the estate. Remember, if the heirs wish to sell the home, they must get lender approval first. Again, the heirs have six months plus two 90-day extensions (generally approved by HUD) for a total of one year to sell the home.

Since I am covering the sale of the home, let me put to rest one of the biggest misconceptions of the reverse mortgage of yesteryear. The lender does not get the home, the lender does not own the home, period. The reverse mortgage is simply a lien on the property that needs to be paid off if any of the events I just covered occur.

CHAPTER FIFTEEN

Can I Sell My Home? A Little More Info

Absolutely yes, anytime. I could say "end of chapter," but let's explore this more. Reverse mortgages do not have a pre-payment penalty, and as I have said, the bank is not going to own your home. If a person wants to sell their home, they can at any time, and the way I seem to be most successful at describing how it works is to compare this to a traditional forward mortgage.

You have a traditional forward mortgage on your home, typically a 30-year fixed rate in today's market. If you sold your home, that mortgage would have to be paid off. You would receive the remaining equity after the mortgage, real estate agent fees (if applicable) and closing costs are paid.

This principal works exactly the same way with a reverse mortgage. You sell your home, the reverse mortgage, real estate agent fees (if applicable) and closing costs are paid. Any remaining equity in the home is yours.

But here is where the similarity stops. On traditional forward mortgages, you are paying principal and interest every month, paying down the mortgage balance. For sake of illustration, let's assume the home value stays the same. As you pay down the forward mortgage you build equity in your home, and when you sell your home, more equity equals more money in your pocket when you sell.

Conversely, with a reverse mortgage the interest and mortgage insurance accrues monthly on the balance of your loan. So, every month you would have less equity in the home and less money in your pocket if you sold your home.

With the understanding that you can sell your home at any time, there are a couple more items to address. First, and for the sake of illustration, my examples above assumed that the home value remained constant. We know this isn't real world and over the long term real estate has appreciated. However, this is a variable over which none of us has control.

Remember the reverse mortgage has the non-recourse feature. If the amount owed on the reverse mortgage ever exceeds the value of the home, the non-recourse provision kicks in and through the mortgage insurance pays the deficit. Conversely, with a traditional forward mortgage, if we have another real estate melt down as we did starting in 2008 and the homeowner finding themselves owing more than the value of the home, there is no non-recourse provision. They are forced to hold on, pay the difference, or face a short-sale or foreclosure.

So yes, and again, you may sell your home at any time. But there are many factors to know and take into consideration when you are looking to obtain a reverse mortgage such that you know your options and obligations when it is time to sell the home. Again, this is why consulting with a reverse mortgage professional is so critical. You want to have a basic understanding of today's reverse mortgage, but it is a complex loan with so many "moving parts" that consulting with a reverse mortgage professional to design the reverse mortgage to best suit your needs and goals can't be emphasized enough.

CHAPTER SIXTEEN

HECMs and Divorce

This is a new chapter in this second addition of the book. Since publishing the first edition, I obtained both **Certified Divorce Lending Professional**[17] **(CDPL) and Certified Mortgage Planning Specialist**[18] **(CMPS)** designations. And why would I get these designations and have them be primary factors to do a second edition to my book?

Well, the baby boomers have cut a new path through life since the beginning. And they are going to keep cutting a new path all the way to the end.

The facts don't lie. Currently, on average, there is a divorce filed in the U.S. every 13 *seconds*: 2.4 million a year. And of all those divorces, divorce is becoming less common for younger adults. However, between 2009 and 2015 the "gray divorce" (those 50 and older) increased 109%[19]. Said differently, in 2015 for every 1,000 married persons age 50 and older, 10 divorced – up from five in 1990. Among people 65 and older, the divorce rate has tripled since 1990 reaching six people per 1,000 married persons in 2015. And there are some downsides to the gray divorcees. Gray divorcees tend to be less financially secure than married and widowed adults, particularly among women.

And I'm not done with the facts. Of all of the divorces, remember one divorce every 13 seconds… 70% involve real estate. 47% either sell or refinance the marital home. Finally, the number of gray divorces is expected to

---

[17] Divorce Lending Institute
[18] Certified Mortgage Planning Specialist Institute
[19] Pew Research Center. Factank. March 9, 2017

continue to increase, from 600,000 in 2009 to an estimated 800,000 per year by 2030[20].

So… given the statistics, divorcing seniors and reverse mortgages is something I have to be very proficient in such that I can best help my senior clients and the professionals that they work with. Understand, I am not an advocate for divorce. However, being aware of these numbers gives cause to a need for a very large number of trained and educated professionals to help divorcing clients as they transition through divorce and into their new lives.

As too often a divorce is seen through a very short term lense: "let's get this over with!" Only months or years down the road someone discovers issue(s) in the Divorce Settlement Agreement that, may not be "wrong" the way the verbiage was written, but it was written in such a way that it wasn't to at least one of the couple's best interest for any one of several reasons.

As a CDLP/CMPS, my job, my commitment, is to share from a residential mortgage planner, a high-level overview of the issues of a divorce as it relates to residential real estate financing. Because in a typical divorce, the couple runs out, hires attorney's and looks at who can screw the other one first, getting it done as soon as possible, and too often it's a fight until the end. Additionally, in addition to the attorney's, there may be a financial advisor, accountant, and quite possibly a realtor involved. And they, while connected to a mutual client, seldom, if ever work together as a team. Adding to this disconnection, are the couple that most likely each one is working with their own different

---

[20] "The Gray Divorce Revolution," Susan Brown and I-Fen, Bowling Green State University

team of professionals. Suddenly, you could have 8 different professionals involved at some level of one couple's divorce and not collaborating. Ouch! So where to begin?

First, when a divorce is filed, it is a lawsuit, until there is a *final* Divorce Settlement Agreement. Subsequently, all lenders with all programs, reverse mortgages included, have special rules they must follow.

Since we are dealing with real estate, let's talk about the value of the home first. Quite likely, it will be the largest asset the couple owns. Subsequently, a fair market value needs to be determined. You would think, "just order an appraisal" and be done with it. Wrong. Most of us, out of shear habit, order an appraisal that is for a mortgage. This type of appraisal is *not* intended to be used for valuation matters other than mortgage financing. There is a specific appraisal to be ordered for a divorce. And one of the features of the divorce appraisal, is the ability to "go back in time". For example, say one spouse moved out six months ago and the attorney wants a value of the home at the time the spouse moved out. A divorce appraisal allows an accurate, relative to time, value of the home, the importance of which cannot be understated.

How the property is owned, and will be owned, is our next topic for discussion. Arizona is a Community property state. Community property is a legal classification of property ownership that applies to certain property, no matter how you hold title to it. Simply stated, it means each spouse owns an undivided one-half of the property. It also has a "Right of Survivorship" clause in it. Meaning, if one spouses passes away, their undivided half is now owned by the surviving spouse and it avoids probate.

A couple getting a divorce may still want to own their marital home together until some event in the future occur. I know several seniors who have school aged children. Perhaps the divorcing couple wants to maintain joint ownership of the marital home until their child is out of school. And a divorce would void the title being held in Community property and converts it to tenancy in common.

Tenancy by the Entirety is the most common way to hold title for a married couple (outside of a Community Property state). Tenancy by the Entirety is a type of concurrent estate in real property held by Husband and Wife whereby each owns the whole of the property coupled with the Right of Survivorship.

Other ways to hold title include Tenancy in Common, Joint Tenancy, Joint Tenancy with Right of Survivorship and a Living Trust. The importance of *how* the property is owned post-divorce must not be overlooked.

How title vesting is to be held post-divorce is something many attorneys overlook. In my example, above where a couple may want to own their marital home after the divorce, let's look at why this is so important. If one spouse remarries, then dies, their new spouse may now own the marital home with the ex-spouse. Likely not the best out-picturing of what anyone had planned.

Knowing the value of the marital home and issues surrounding title (ownership), now let's look at some areas where a reverse mortgage could really come into play and benefit the senior couple getting a divorce.

A divorcing senior couple may have virtually all their assets in their home. Subsequently, to equally divide their assets, it may force the sale of their home at a time when, for many reasons, that may not be the best decision. I had a client, a gentleman in his eighty's. He was going through a very challenging divorce and owed his ex-spouse $120,000 to settle the divorce. He would have had to sell many of his things to downsize, as he could no longer afford to buy the size of home he currently had and sell the home to pay off his ex. I truly was worried for his health during the process of getting a reverse mortgage. With a reverse mortgage, I was able to get him the funds to pay of his ex-wife. I literally saw him physical change (for the better) as we walked out of the closing.

The first area to consider a reverse mortgage may simply be to have the ability for one spouse to stay in the marital home and give the other spouse their share of equity.

Another common area that needs to be addressed with divorcing seniors is the retirement plan. Too often, one spouse has worked and accumulated a substantial retirement account, often a 401k. And/or there may be a substantial brokerage account that needs to be divided. Let's assume this couple has a home that has no mortgage on it. It *may* be more beneficial, assuming the spouse staying in the home has these assets, to obtain a reverse mortgage to pay their ex, in lieu of taking funds out of a retirement or brokerage account. This is one of many scenario's I could use to show how utilizing a reverse mortgage can be used relating to assets in a divorce situation. Let's talk about income next.

Say one spouse has not worked for decades. Now they may be in their seventies and because of the divorce, they need a monthly income. Add to this, there could, yes in a gray divorce, be child support to be paid to an ex-spouse. Assuming the divorcing spouse that would owe maintenance/alimony/child support and is staying in the marital home, they may be able to obtain a monthly income equal to the amount that they need to pay their ex monthly.

Another area of potential concern is capital gains taxes. Albeit, this isn't only relating to the marital home. It may be relating to an investment property or properties that need to be sold per the Divorce Settlement Agreement. For the spouse staying the marital home, or the ex could have purchased a new home and have substantial equity, they could obtain a reverse mortgage to pay capital gains taxes, thereby being able to keep their share of net proceeds from the sale of the property/properties in "cash" and let the reverse mortgage pay the taxes.

The last area I will touch on is liabilities. A couple married for decades could have a long list of joint accounts. Taking these apart through a divorce can be challenging and time consuming. Yet it needs to be done. Each spouse needs to be very vigilant in handling these accounts and not paying a bill out of spite today can have lasting negative consequences to both spouses for years to come.

I have but touched the tip of the proverbial iceberg on this subject. And with hundreds of thousands of gray divorces happening each year, and the numbers are rising, and seniors have trillions of dollars of equity sitting in their homes in the U.S., this is a growing market that needs specialists on all fronts to ensure the divorcing couple's needs are taking care of not only through the divorce, but especially in the case of a gray divorce, for the rest of their lives.

Perhaps the biggest take away in this chapter is knowing a divorcing couple with substantial equity in their home can, and many more should than do, look into a reverse mortgage as a financial planning tool to utilize and leverage in being able to settle their divorce.

I have my soapbox for reverse mortgages. Please allow me a divorce soapbox too. Divorces require special knowledge in the mortgage lending arena. Reverse mortgages require special knowledge that, relatively speaking, very few have in our industry. Couple divorce with reverse mortgage and you *need a seasoned, professional that is a specialist in both areas.* A divorcing senior couple utilizing a reverse mortgage in my professional opinion, I can't think of a more difficult loan scenario! And a reverse mortgage may be the best financial tool for a spouse in a gray divorce to obtain. This option shouldn't be ignored because of complexity. You don't trust having an open-heart surgery to a general practitioner doctor, don't trust this issue to a general loan officer! The divorcing gray couple doesn't have decades (in all likelihood) to make up for costly mistakes made by an ignorant mortgage lender.

CHAPTER SEVENTEEN

What is Financial Assessment?

Prior to the financial crisis that started in 2008, to obtain a reverse mortgage, you needed to have equity in your home and be able to breathe fog on a mirror. That was pretty much the extent of qualifying for your reverse mortgage, as no formal underwriting was required. But alas, the financial crisis caused a major overhaul in reverse mortgages and one of those major overhauls was the creation and implementation of Financial Assessment that became effective March 2, 2015[21]. Remember from Chapter 3, Financial Assessment is HUD's term for underwriting. And remember, HECM's are *not* underwritten like any traditional forward mortgage!

Let me first cover why financial assessment was born, because many people ask, "Why does my credit or income matter, because I don't have a house payment?" (Actually, you don't have a *principal and interest payment*.)

Basically, HUD's concern and answer is they want to assure the homeowner (the borrower) that after the reverse mortgage is taken out the borrower has enough discretionary income (HUD calls it *residual income*) to pay their property charges (taxes, insurance, etc.), their monthly bills, and maintain a minimum discretionary income that HUD sets for individuals and couples. In other words, what's the point of obtaining a reverse mortgage if you are going to be (or remain) in financial trouble?

In HUD's own words; "[T]he mortgagee must evaluate the mortgagor's willingness and capacity to timely meet his or

---

[21] HUD Mortgagee Letter 2014-21

her financial obligations and to comply with the mortgage requirements. In conducting this financial assessment, mortgagees must take into consideration that some mortgagors seek a HECM due to financial difficulties, which may be reflected in the mortgagor's credit report and/or property charge payment history. The mortgagee must also consider to what extent the proceeds of the HECM could provide a solution to any such financial difficulties."[22]

Simply stated, it comes down to two things: capacity and willingness. Let me do a little translation for you.

Borrower's capacity translates to income. Willingness translates to credit. A little sidebar here. Before credit reports as we know them today, lenders based their credit decisions on the "Three C's". And the second "C" was Character. If a person was of good character, they would definitely pay their bills. Interesting, to me, how we are almost going full circle with this one. A person's willingness to pay their bills can be seen as a reflection of their character.

Here is how HUD defines and uses the terms *capacity* and *willingness*. As I just said, capacity translates to income. The HECM product looks at a person's income to determine if they have enough monthly income to pay their property charges (see below), monthly debts such as a car payment, and have some money each month to live on. These are the areas they look at related to their home:

1. Real estate taxes
2. Homeowners Insurance

---

[22] HECM Financial Assessment and Property Charge Guide

3. Other property charges: condo associations, flood insurance, assessment fees, etc.
4. Reverse mortgages also calculate against your residual income 14 cents per square foot to cover the cost of utilities.

It doesn't stop there. Also calculated in this capacity formula are other monthly obligations such as a car payment, student loan payment (yes, seniors have student loans) and credit card minimum monthly payments. Simply stated, taking a borrower(s) gross monthly income and subtracting these expenses, the lender wants to see approximately $1,100 in discretionary income for a couple and $600 for an individual. I say, "simply stated", as HUD provides a table and based on the family size and region they live in the U.S. to determine the required residual income. It varies across the U.S. from $529 to over $1,100[23]. Additionally, there are rules and exceptions to who you count. Again, this augments the importance of talking to a reverse mortgage specialist to insure it is being calculated correctly!

This gives you a good, basic, and *very* high-level understanding of capacity / income. Let's move onto the willingness / credit section for a better understanding of what the underwriter is going to look for.

Again, in HUD's own words regarding willingness and what they are focused on: "The purpose of the credit history analysis is to determine if the mortgagor (borrower) has demonstrated responsible management of debt, finances, and homeownership obligations. The mortgagee

---

[23] HECM Financial Assessment and Property Charge Guide, Effective for HECM case numbers issued on or after January, 13, 2014. Section 3.12

(lender) must analyze the mortgagor's credit history and loan application to identify debts/obligations that must be included in the residual income analysis and to determine if the mortgagor has:

- Delinquent Federal debt
- Any unpaid liens against the subject property resulting from a State or court-ordered judgments;
- A satisfactory payment history on revolving credit, installment accounts, and mortgages; and
- A satisfactory history of timely payment of property charges"[24]

Allow me to do more translation. Again, credit / willingness / character. A borrower may have the money but demonstrate a lack of responsibility to pay their bills. This may be because they simply are not a responsible person, in which case the chances of obtaining any loan gets mighty slim. I believe most of the time a person has the willingness, but a life event took place, i.e., a major illness or the death of a spouse. In such case, there may be valid reasons and the borrower could still obtain the reverse mortgage.

Then there is LESA (pronounced Lisa). LESA stands for Life Expectancy Set Aside. The reverse mortgage underwriter is going to perform two tests: a credit and property charge payment test and a residual income test. If the borrower fails one or both tests, a LESA may be required to be able to approve the loan. I cover the LESA in dept in Chapter 22.

---

[24] HECM Financial Assessment and Property Charge Guide

In summary, financial assessment on a reverse mortgage is not, nor is it designed to be, a "hard" yes or no approval of a reverse mortgage loan. With compensating factors and/or extenuating circumstances coupled with a LESA, a borrower may still qualify for a reverse mortgage. Since the inception of the financial assessment rule, fewer borrowers have qualified for a reverse mortgage. On the positive side of this, the homeowners who do qualify are better qualified borrowers. They are better qualified to stay in their home, maintain their home, and the federal government is insuring higher quality loans. Said differently, the new path HECMs are on is a path of win – win – win. A win for current homeowners, as they are getting a financially stronger loan. A win for the lender, as they have a better book of business. Remember, a better book of business for lenders translates into lower rates and fees for the borrowers. And finally, a win for future borrowers. As HECMs continue to prove themselves and are used more as a retirement planning tool, the HECMs of tomorrow will continue to evolve into a better loan.

CHAPTER EIGHTEEN

How a HECM Matures

As a society, we are trained to think "30-year mortgage." You get a 30-year mortgage, work hard, and pay it off. Only then do you have no mortgage payment. Forget what you know—this is the land of reverse mortgages.

Reverse mortgages have no maturity or end date. Conceptually, if a person lived to be 120 years old and lived in their home, God bless them, they have a reverse mortgage that is still at work for them.

But HECMs do mature. And there are various reasons they do. These are called "Maturity Events," and when a maturity event occurs[25], the loan becomes due and payable. Here is the list of Maturity Events:

- The home must be the principal residence of one of the borrowers. In the event of the death of one of the spouses, as long as the surviving spouse remains in the home and it is their primary residence, all is good, as it is still a primary residence for one of the borrowers. In the event of a single person, obviously, if it was no longer their primary residence, this provision would "trip" and the loan would be due and payable.

(Refer to Chapter 14 for additional information on the death of a borrower.)

- If for a period of longer than 12 consecutive months a borrower fails to occupy the home as their primary residence due to physical or mental illness

---

[25] HUD Handbook 4235.1 Chapter 13

and there is no spouse, the loan would become due and payable. An example of this is if one spouse needed to go into an assisted living facility. They no longer reside at the subject property. This does not trip a maturity event if the other spouse still maintains the home as their primary residence.

- The obligations of the homeowner to maintain the property is not upheld. This is defined as paying property taxes, homeowner's insurance, and other property charges, in addition to the borrower maintaining the property in good condition.
- The borrower cannot sell the property or convey title to the property.

There are special provisions for a non-borrowing spouse (see Chapter 12 for non-borrowing spouse).

HECM Maturity Events are pretty straightforward: non-primary residence (some form of that as outlined above) or failure to maintain the home. And don't think lenders give you a loan today and sit back and watch the interest accrue, counting the days before they get their money. Far from it!

Lenders do due diligence in making sure these Maturity Events are not occurring and borrowers or heirs are not letting them know. This includes annual phone calls to the borrowers to confirm they are still alive and living in their home. A letter is sent annually to the borrower which includes a questionnaire that needs to be completed and returned to the lender. This is done for the same reason as the phone calls. Also, lenders send people out to take pictures of homes. Remember, this is a federally insured loan and the collateral for the loan is the borrower's home. It is in everyone's best interest to keep claims against the insurance fund low. A property well maintained ensures the homeowner and the lender that if the home needed to be sold, they would get market value and not have to discount the sales price because the home needed repairs.

Again, this is good for the lender, as a home in good condition will sell quicker and for more money. And this is equally good for the homeowner. It is also in all homeowners' best interest to live in a home that has no health and safety issues. This includes *around* the property, not only *in* the property.

I tried to do a reverse mortgage for a brother and sister who lived together. They had come to me, and I had not been to their home. All looked good until the appraisal came back: they were hoarders! I did end up going to their home and, being my first experience with hoarding, I was shocked. The brother couldn't give up his newspapers and magazines and there were literally paths through the home to walk on. Stacks of magazines and newspapers on chairs, tables, and the floor. He had been collecting them for decades!

The sad ending to this story is he could not give up his newspapers and magazines and they didn't go through with the loan. But think of the health and safety issues in their home! God forbid a fire should break out, with all that fuel for a fire. And who knows what is crawling around in the home, as I am sure some areas hadn't been cleaned in decades. Health and safety was a major issue with them and think of the salability of the home.

If that home was to be sold, someone would have to clean it out and clean it up, and this isn't happening for free in any real estate market. Therefore, the value of the home would be substantially less not only because of the hoarding issue, but also because all the stuff in the home prevented anyone from knowing if the need for repairs even existed.

It was very sad for me to see anyone living as this brother and sister did. Yet their situation will serve me for years as an extreme example of health and safety issues that the HECM world is committed to assuring do not exist for a borrower with a reverse mortgage.

CHAPTER NINETEEN

Why Do I Have to Pay Mortgage Insurance?

First, know mortgage insurance must be paid, no way around it. But it is a good thing and let me explain why. First, let's look at the traditional forward mortgage world, the world in which we learned about mortgages. If you don't have a 20% down payment with a traditional forward mortgage, you will need to pay for private mortgage insurance. And whose interest does it serve? The lenders! It isn't for your best interest. The lender makes you buy insurance in case you default on your loan, so they can make an insurance claim and the insurance pays for any *deficiency* (the amount between the loan amount and the sales price, including expenses) that they are short. Conversely, mortgage insurance on a HECM is in *the borrower's* best interest.

With a HECM loan, you are required to pay mortgage insurance upfront, Initial Mortgage Insurance Premium (IMIP). Effective October 2, 2017, HUD changed the fees for both the IMIP and the monthly insurance[26].

The IMIP factor is applied to the *value of the home, not the loan amount*. Effective October 2, 2017, the IMIP is 2% regardless of the percentage of principal limit you receive at closing[27].

Additionally, the annual mortgage insurance premium is one-half of one percent (0.5%). The annual mortgage insurance premium is charged to the outstanding principal balance monthly.

---

[26] HUD Mortgagee Letter 2017-12

[27] HUD Mortgagee Letter 2017-12

HECM loans are federally insured loans, through FHA. FHA has a separate account, called the *Mutual Mortgage Insurance Fund (MMIF)* into which the mortgage insurance is paid and then the MMIF is used to pay out insurance claims. And FHA designed the rates of the MMIF with no profit margin designed into them for the Federal government.

Now that you understand *what* you have to pay, let me explain *why* you have to pay. And why I believe mortgage insurance on a HECM is a good thing.

Allow me to take it to the bottom line on *why* you pay mortgage insurance and back into it from there. Why you pay mortgage insurance is to insure the functionality of your reverse mortgage for the life of the loan. There are several ways that can play out… let me explain.

- For borrowers who have a "tenure monthly payment," aka a set monthly income for life, the mortgage insurance guarantees the continuance of the monthly income for the borrower's life, regardless of the value of the home.
- For borrowers with a "term monthly income," aka a set monthly income for a set number of years, the mortgage insurance guarantees the payment of the monthly income for the term set regardless of the value of the home.

While not as likely to happen with the term monthly income, it is a real possibility that with a tenure monthly income the borrower could more than exhaust the equity in their home if they live a long life. Again, if the borrower becomes "upside down," owing more than the value of their home, they will continue to get their monthly income.

98

- For borrowers who have a line of credit, contractually the line of credit with a reverse mortgage *grows* monthly for as long as the borrower is in their home and no maturity events are triggered. If a borrower took out a line of credit at the age of 62 and lived to be 100, the initial line of credit amount would be over *4 times* the initial line of credit amount. For example, a $120,000 line of credit today could grow to over $400,000[28] by the time the borrower is 90 years old. Add to that any initial amount used to pay off a mortgage and you can quickly see how large the HECM loan balance could be. The mortgage insurance guarantees that the proceeds in the line of credit, as it grows, is available to the homeowner, regardless of the value of the home.

There is also a modified tenure and a modified term loan, which combines the monthly payment option with the line of credit. These two combinations obviously have the same capacity to grow the loan balance to the point of exceeding the value of the home. Again, this is why you have the mortgage insurance: to cover the deficit.

Remember the non-recourse provision? Let's combine the non-recourse provision with the mortgage insurance and bring this home.

If the loan goes "upside down," aka, the loan amount exceeds the value of the home, the non-recourse provision coupled with the mortgage insurance "kicks in." *The mortgage insurance is how the FHA can guarantee the*

---

[28] Based on a hypothetical scenario using an assumed rate on 11.12.17 For illustration and educational purposes only.

non-recourse provision. What does that mean to the borrower and their children or estate?

This is a BIG deal, so please pay attention! It means that Mom and Dad will go to their grave with the peace of mind they did not leave debt to their children. It means the children will not inherit any debt. It means that, regardless of the size of the estate, only the home can be used as collateral against the HECM loan. Said differently, the lender isn't coming after the bank account or the estate to make up the shortage of how much the loan was "upside down!"

This type of mortgage insurance is unique to the HECM. It needs to be understood and, once understood, you can see why it is a very good feature of the HECM. In fact, between the non-recourse feature, which can happen because of the insurance, and the line of credit feature, these are two primary reasons reverse mortgages today are being used more as a retirement planning tool.

CHAPTER TWENTY

You CAN Make Mortgage Payments!

For years, reverse mortgages have been touted as "you never have to make a mortgage payment." That statement is incorrect. You don't *have to* make a principal and interest payment. But you always have to pay your real estate taxes, homeowner's insurance, flood insurance, and homeowner's association dues. Now that we have that understanding, let's move on to the fact that you *can* make payments on a HECM loan and why you may want to.

This is a fact that, unfortunately, even some mortgage professionals don't know and a whole lot of seniors don't know! Sadly, this causes potentially missing a great opportunity to utilize and maximize some of the advantages of a reverse mortgage.

We know that if no principal and interest payments are made on a reverse mortgage, the interest and mortgage insurance accrues monthly on the principal balance. In short, every month your loan balance increases. The first potential benefit of making a payment is to reduce the loan balance. And, as with any loan, reduction of the principal loan amount decreases the amount of interest and mortgage insurance accruing on the loan. This serves to protect the homeowner's equity since they will owe less on their mortgage.

One critical factor to know with a reverse mortgage: in paying down the loan balance, paying off the reverse mortgage is **not** recommended! The recommendation is to pay the loan balance down to not less than $100. Keeping the minimum balance on the loan does two things. First, it keeps your reverse mortgage active. Second, it preserves the line of credit, potentially the biggest feature of a reverse mortgage.

An additional benefit of making payments, especially to the younger borrower, is the possible tax benefit. For example, if a person is still working and needs or wants the tax write-off, making payments allocated toward mortgage insurance and/or mortgage interest may have beneficial tax considerations. The loan servicer would send the borrower a Form 1098 in January following the year the payments were made.

Now here is the biggest secret of making a payment on your reverse mortgage… drum roll… the potential increase in the available line of credit. The line of credit feature is fast becoming the number one reason financial advisors across the country are recommending reverse mortgages. Remember, a HECM Line of Credit contractually grows every month. By making payments and reducing the principal balance, you increase the availability of funds on your line of credit. And any reduction in the loan balance will have a corresponding increase in the line of credit. Let me put one more layer on this, then go full circle and come back to this issue of paying down a line of credit.

Let's address making periodic payments to a reverse mortgage. Making periodic payments can be accomplished in a couple of ways. First, if a person is still actively working, they may from time to time "chunk down" the principal balance from their earnings. The second possibility is when investments mature or are sold off. Taking all or part of those investments and paying down the loan balance is yet another option. There is also a third option. Many baby-boomers in their 60's and even 70's have parents still alive. This is the foundation of my third option: an inheritance. Taking some or all of an inheritance and further reducing the loan balance.

Going full circle, whether payments are made as in my first explanation of why you would pay down a principal balance or the principal balance is decreased in any one or more of the periodic payment methods I just described, this leads to a corresponding increase in the available funds on a line of credit.

Now knowing that you *can* make payments on a reverse mortgage, your reverse mortgage just became a financial planning tool. This is when it is advisable to work with *both* a reverse mortgage specialist and a financial advisor. Let them work together to determine what is best for *you*. This is something that needs to happen far more than it currently does. With more financial advisors becoming educated in reverse mortgages, my hope is that collaboration and cooperation between these two professions will happen a lot more… a very good thing.

CHAPTER TWENTY-ONE

Purchase a Home with a Reverse Mortgage: H4P

I truly believe this is a sleeper! Not many mortgage professionals, real estate agents, builders, financial advisors, or the public know you can purchase a home using a reverse mortgage. In part, the reason for this is about the time HUD approved HECMs for purchase, more commonly known as H4P, the U.S. economy was in a severe recession. The Housing and Economic Recovery Act of 2008 (HERA)[29] provides HECM mortgagors with the opportunity to purchase a principal residence with HECM proceeds. HERA became effective January 1, 2009.

You can see why not a lot of people cared at the time. Too many people were concerned about just keeping their homes! Real estate agents were into learning about and doing short-sales and foreclosure transactions. Financial planners were watching the net worth of their clients disappear. But today we are in different times.

H4Ps are a different animal from a refinance reverse mortgage... *way different!* I don't mean a lot more paperwork, how the loan is calculated, or general underwriting rules. What I mean is there are relatively small things in number, but those small things can make for a denied loan weeks after the application and/or a very challenging closing if the loan is not structured correctly! For those reasons, I am really "on it" with this topic. Mistakes here can be costly: you have many parties involved and there are more "moving parts" to a purchase transaction.

---

[29] Mortgagee Letter 2008-33

I have said, more than once, how important it is to consult with a reverse mortgage specialist: someone who has experience with reverse mortgages. With a H4P, it is even more important to consult with a seasoned reverse mortgage professional. Over 95% of all reverse mortgages done are refinance transactions. Many reverse mortgage professionals have never done a purchase transaction and they have been in the business several years. I am not diminishing anyone for not having done a H4P, but I am saying that they are different than a refinance transaction and ideally you want a reverse mortgage professional who has experience in doing a H4P.

Let me highlight this program and call out the unique aspects of this loan. First, and simply stated, it is a reverse mortgage. There is nothing different about that simple fact. The guidelines for qualifying and underwriting guidelines are the same as with a refinance transaction. However, HUD has an additional set of underwriting guidelines regarding H4P transactions! And, worth noting, the underwriting guidelines for a H4P in ways are more liberal than a traditional forward purchase mortgage.

You have sellers, buyers, real estate agents, and a title and escrow company, involved with this transaction. More parties to the transaction, and an additional set of underwriting guidelines to "operate" under. Primary reasons you need a reverse mortgage specialist to handle these transactions!

People often are confused or simply don't understand how you can purchase a home with a reverse mortgage. Again, let me compare it to a traditional forward mortgage. With a traditional forward mortgage, you purchase a home and you typically need a down payment. For example, you purchase a $300,000 home and put out 10% ($30,000) as a down payment. The lender provides a mortgage loan for $270,000. Now you bought your home, you own the home, and you have a traditional *forward mortgage lien* on the property. And you have a principal and interest payment to make.

Using the same purchase price of $300,000, only this time purchasing a home with a reverse mortgage, and assuming you're 70 years old, you would need a down payment of 51.4% or $154,200[30]. The lender would provide the reverse mortgage loan of $145,800. Now you bought your home, you own the home, and you have a *reverse mortgage lien* on the property. With a reverse mortgage, no principal and interest payment needs to be made.

There are a few scenarios I want to share to illustrate the benefits of utilizing a reverse mortgage to purchase a home. The first scenario is for borrowers who are downsizing. Say they sold their home for $400,000 (and had no mortgage balance). They want to purchase a smaller home for $250,000, their retirement dream home. Initially they were planning on taking the $250,000 from the $400,000 they received from the sale of their home to purchase their new home. $250,000 of their $400,000 "gone," invested in their new home.

Utilizing a reverse mortgage, there would be a $125,000 down payment to purchase their $250,000 home[31]. There are two benefits to this strategy. First is the additional $125,000 not spent on the acquisition of their home,

---

[30] This example is ONLY for the sake of education and illustration. PLF as of 11.12.17. Actual down payment determined by age of youngest borrower. Additionally, I have not taken into account loan program, closing costs, rates, etc.
[31] For simplicity, illustration, and to serve as an example, I used a 50% down payment. Down payment will vary depending on age and other factors.

leaving additional funds for their retirement fund, to invest, to check off items on a bucket list, or whatever the money is best spent for. The second benefit is there is no principal and interest payment that must be made. No principal and interest payment means additional cash flow for their retirement years.

Let me offer the second scenario. Say a couple sold their home for $250,000 and came looking to buy a new home. They are thinking they have $250,000 to spend. Wrong! With a reverse mortgage, they could purchase a $400,000 - $500,000 home![32]. Imagine how happy a retired couple would be to know they could potentially *double their purchase price and have no principal and interest payment!*

Or say they found that almost perfect $250,000 home with a builder selling homes in the $225,000 to $350,000 price point. With a reverse mortgage, they could now afford upgrades and/or a larger model of home, whereas, if all they had to spend was the $250,000, they are limited.

Yet another scenario. With $250,000, buyers are limited to the cash they have. Utilizing a reverse mortgage opens them up to more inventory to choose from. And "moving up" is never hard to do. Especially when they may not be using all of their funds to do it and they don't have a principal and interest payment.

Last scenario that I will call the advanced one. A senior homeowner can "over fund" the purchase and simultaneously create a line of credit. Again, this is the "advanced" loan, so consult with a reverse mortgage specialist for details on this option.

---

[32] See footnotes 26 & 27

Keep in mind, my examples are for educational and illustration purposes only and actual figures will vary.

Another factor that enters into this equation of making the H4P program a great loan today is the interest rate and fees associated with the loan. As of October 2, 2017, HUD *lowered* the interest rates on reverse mortgages. Additionally, they *lowered* the upfront mortgage insurance (relative to a purchase transaction) and the annual mortgage insurance. Lower interest rates coupled with lower fees… making it more economical to utilize a reverse mortgage for a purchase transaction.

Beginning to see why I said this was a sleeper? **This loan makes retirement dreams come true!**

Continuing this conversation, let's look at the details of turning dreams into reality. Since this is a purchase transaction, let's look at property types first. Eligible property types are:

- Existing single-family homes, more than one year old
- Existing single-family homes less than one year old, where a Certificate of Occupancy or its equivalent has been issued.
- Manufactured homes built after June 15, 1976 that have never been moved and meet all FHA requirements. (Many people don't know you can finance manufactured homes with a reverse mortgage.)
- Modular homes
- FHA approved condos
- 2 – 4 unit properties

Knowing what types of properties can be financed and understanding the specifics of the financing component is critical. And worth noting, as with all reverse mortgages, the property must be the borrower's primary residence. HUD requires the home to be occupied within 60 days of closing. That said, let me take this apart and look at each component.

Obtaining counseling. In any reverse mortgage transaction, the borrower(s) needs to obtain counseling. With a purchase transaction, the address on the counseling certificate needs to be the borrower's existing home address, not the property being considered for purchase or, in the case of new construction, the new home address.

There needs to be a fully executed sales contract (all parties have signed the contract). There are additional forms in the sales contract that need to be completed as well. Consult your reverse mortgage specialist to obtain the most current list of forms. Also, the transaction needs to be a "non-arm's length" transaction, meaning the buyer and seller are uninterested parties. And HUD has very specific flipping guidelines. If the seller has recently purchased the home and is now selling it, expect additional requirements or a loan denial.

All properties must meet FHA's minimum property requirements to qualify for a HECM purchase loan. If an appraiser, inspector, engineer, or termite company identifies issues with the property, the SELLER must complete the repairs at their expense and before closing. FHA's objective is two-fold. First is to protect the senior homeowner. They are looking at health and safety issues, the security of the property, and the soundness of the structure. Additionally, keep in mind that reverse mortgages are collateral guaranteed loans (the non-recourse provision), so FHA wants to also insure that the property (their collateral) is in good shape.

As I stated in the beginning of this chapter, I believe this loan is a sleeper! My hope is that through education and marketing of this program, more people will take advantage of the H4P program. And to continue to repeat myself, this program needs a reverse mortgage professional to guide the process and insure the correct documents are executed and things are done in the correct sequence. It can be used as a stand-alone product and also as a retirement planning tool. Either way and with all of this said, this loan is a great product.

CHAPTER TWENTY-TWO

Fixed or Adjustable Rate?

I'm going to repeat myself again: "it depends" is my answer. Reverse mortgages have two primary programs to choose from: a fixed rate or an adjustable rate loan[33]. You always have a choice between the two, but there are clear disadvantages and clear advantages to each program depending upon the goals of the borrower and the purpose for which the loan is being used. And in every reverse mortgage presentation, the lender (the Reverse Mortgage Specialist) must show you a *minimum of three options*. And one of the options must be the fixed rate product. The other two products are the monthly adjustable and annual adjustable rate programs.

But the bottom line and the right choice comes down to the program you, the borrower, are comfortable with that best fits your needs and goals. Knowing the bottom line, let's dive into this so you can make an educated and informed decision.

Fixed rate HECMs are the vast *minority* of the reverse mortgages taken, with good reason. And just like a traditional forward mortgage, *fixed rate* means the rate is fixed for the life of the loan. We are now so used to getting a fixed rate traditional forward mortgage that most people automatically think they should get a fixed rate for their reverse mortgage. Most likely not, and it is time for a new perspective.

The reason you likely will not want the fixed rate HECM is because when you close on this loan, you are done getting

---

[33] HUD Mortgagee Letter 2007-13

any future equity from your home... *done*. Remember all those options? Tenure, or term payments, additional cash withdraws, line of credit? They go away, are not available, with a fixed rate HECM. However, there may be times when you want to get a fixed rate HECM. And I can think of two scenarios where you may want to choose, or at least consider, the fixed rate option.

First, if you are refinancing your home, paying off your existing traditional forward mortgage with a reverse mortgage, and if you are taking almost all or all your available proceeds from the new HECM to pay off your existing mortgage. Since additional equity is not available as you have "tapped out" all available funds on the HECM to get the loan, term or tenure payments, additional cash, or a line of credit are not, nor will they ever be, available to you.

What if you were refinancing your existing traditional forward mortgage with a HECM and, for the sake of example, there was $50,000 available for a line of credit. Remember, the line of credit *grows* in value monthly, so the $50,000 is *today's value*. And instead of taking an adjustable rate HECM, which I will cover next, you choose to take a fixed rate HECM. One way of looking at this is you just left $50,000 in your home for as long as you have your reverse mortgage. If you take a fixed rate HECM, that $50,000 line of credit is NOT available to you. It is a line of credit that you *may* tap into in the future, but with the fixed rate you just gave up your option to that option. Not necessarily a bad choice, but just know what you did before you sign up for a fixed rate HECM.

The other scenario is the H4P, purchasing a home with a reverse mortgage. With a HECM purchase, you are using all available funds from the HECM to purchase the home. Virtually every time all the available funds from the H4P are used to purchase the home. In the case where all the funds are NOT used at closing, and this is using a HECM as a retirement planning tool such that additional funds are paid at the closing to establish a line of credit, ignore this scenario and talk to your reverse mortgage specialist to understand this option better.

Assuming with a H4P that you are using all of the available funds to purchase your home, this is the other scenario when you may want to consider a fixed rate HECM. Again, having used all available funds at closing, no term or tenure payments or line of credit are or ever will be available. With both scenarios I just shared with you, the important element in each one is that all available HECM proceeds were taken at the closing of the loan. This negates any future withdraws of equity and therefore a fixed rate can now be considered.

New conversation: Adjustable Rate HECM loans or HECM-ARM (Adjustable Rate Mortgage). There are two of them to discuss and they should always be shown to you when you are considering a HECM loan (in addition to the fixed rate product). I said it was time for a new perspective, and the time has come as the vast *majority* of HECM loans today are adjustable rate loans... and for VERY good reasons.

But first, let me explain the basics of adjustable rate mortgages and how they work. *ALL* adjustable rate mortgages are comprised of two components: an index and a margin. The *index* is the variable in the "adjustable" rate. Currently, HECM loans are using the LIBOR index, but HUD is looking to stop using the LIBOR by 2020. No replacement index has been named, but they have a few to choose from and I am confident they will find a replacement and things will continue smoothly going forward.

As with any adjustable rate mortgage, you always want to research and see what the index historically has done. While this is no indication of the future and what it may do, it is a good representation of what it *likely* will do. And this advice isn't for only when you are looking to get a reverse mortgage and you want to know what it has been. For as long as you have an HECM-ARM, you can look to see what the index is doing. Find the current index rate, add your margin (a life of loan constant) and you would know, if your rate was adjusting today, what it would adjust to. I find knowing this gives peace of mind to people, as they can stay current with what their rate is doing.

Let's continue with the index conversation. Both HECM adjustable rate products currently use the LIBOR index. The difference between the two is whether the rate adjusts *annually* or *monthly*. When an adjustable rate adjusts, there are two components to look at regarding the adjustment. First is the annual "cap" or limit the loan can increase per year. The second is the "cap" or limit the loan can increase by over the life of the loan.

Historically, the annual caps have been 2%. This means from the rate you start at, that rate cannot increase more than 2% per year from your initial rate. But for how long can it increase? This is called the "lifetime cap," which is the lifetime ceiling of how high the interest rate could go. Historically, the *monthly* adjustable LIBOR HECM-ARM has had a lifetime cap 10% over the initial or beginning rate. In comparison, the LIBOR HECM-ARM *annual* adjustable program has had a lifetime cap 5% over the initial or beginning rate.

I just shared with you the two adjustable HECM-ARM products: the *annual* adjustable rate program and the *monthly* adjustable rate program. The product names tell you when the interest rates are going to adjust. The monthly adjustable HECM-ARM will adjust the interest rate monthly, while the annual adjustable HECM-ARM will adjust the interest rate annually. Please note these two programs, in addition to having substantially different lifetime caps, may also have different initial rates. When looking at and comparing these products, make sure you are comparing *the same expected rates on both products!*

Speaking of margins, it brings us to the second component in an adjustable rate mortgage: the margin. The margin is the constant in an adjustable rate mortgage. Once it is set, it is locked for the life of the loan. Add the margin to the index and you have the interest rate you are paying. You would begin your HECM loan with an initial (or beginning) interest rate and it will be good for the initial term of the loan. For an annual HECM-ARM, the initial interest rate is what you will pay for the first year (the initial term). For the monthly HECM-ARM, the initial rate is what you will pay for the first month (the initial term).

Now you know the basics of an adjustable rate mortgage. And you know there are two different adjustable rates offered plus the one fixed rate product. So, you should always get the lowest rate for your HECM loan, correct? Not necessarily! This is one of the major components in why you should always deal with a reverse mortgage specialist and not a traditional forward mortgage professional.

Getting the lowest interest rate on a HECM mortgage *may not be in your best interest* (no pun intended)! For people who have a line of credit, the growth rate of the line of credit is your interest rate plus the mortgage insurance rate. Having the lowest possible interest rate today could cost you tens of thousands of dollars in the future value of your line of credit at a time when you would likely need it the most. Keep in mind the value of the line of credit is NOT tied into the value of your home. It grows regardless of the value of your home.

Conversely, if you have a large traditional forward mortgage you are paying off and a small line of credit, you may want to go for a lower interest rate. As the majority of interest is charged on the outstanding balance of the loan, and since that line of credit represents a small percentage of the total loan balance, this strategy may be best. Also, having a small line of credit balance initially, a relatively small difference in your interest rate may not make that much difference in future value of your line of credit. This approach may be the best because it gives you a lower interest rate on the largest amount of money while still providing you a line of credit for possible future use.

In summary on a HECM-ARM, the index (variable) plus your margin (constant) equals your rate. This rate becomes your initial rate, determines your lifetime cap interest rate, and is the major component of the interest rate used for your line of credit growth.

Understanding *how* an adjustable rate works, let's look at *why* you would get one. The HECM-ARM is *the only product that allows you to get to more of your home's equity in the future (after you have closed on your HECM loan). Period.* This is the loan that is used as a financial planning tool.

In Chapter 5, I covered the various ways you can utilize a reverse mortgage to pull the equity from your property. And I want to again highlight those options for you as they relate to a HECM-ARM. Also, in the next chapter I will be discussing the LESA. But I want to include a brief discussion here because it is fitting for the HECM-ARM product.

As an example, let's say you are looking to get a reverse mortgage and if you have an existing mortgage to pay off, let's assume it is small. So, what you have is a larger percentage of your home equity to tap into. This is where you work with a reverse mortgage specialist and perhaps your accountant and/or financial advisor to determine the best way to structure your HECM-ARM. Given the amount of equity available, you can choose from the following options:

- **Term payment** – a fixed monthly payment for a fixed time period (term), or
- **Tenure payment** – a fixed monthly payment for your life
- **Line of Credit** – contractually grows monthly for the life of loan unless utilized and then any remaining unused portion continues to grow monthly
- **Modified Term** – a combination of a term payment and a line of credit
- **Modified Tenure** – a combination of a tenure payment and a line of credit
- **Cash-Out** - A lump sum cash distribution.

Any one of these six options can be utilized with a HECM-ARM, again, given you have enough equity. These five options are NOT available with a fixed rate HECM. The options are *critical* in using a HECM for a retirement planning tool. And this is the "why" you get a HECM-ARM instead of a fixed rate HECM.

Additionally, there may be a LESA. *LESA* stands for *Life Expectancy Set Aside* and simply stated is a forced escrow account set up by the lender to pay future real estate taxes and homeowners insurance. I cover LESAs in depth in Chapter 22.

Now you have a basic understanding of the fixed rate HECM and the two HECM-ARMs, plus the knowing that there is this "thing" called a LESA. My advice with a HECM-ARM is don't be afraid of it. You know now that you can study the index and what it has done. Additionally, you can look up the index any time you want and see what it is doing, then add your margin to it, and you'll know what your interest rate is doing. To know and understand this is just good financial sense. But don't lose sight of why you are getting the reverse mortgage in the first place. And without exception, getting a reverse mortgage comes down to peace of mind and quality of life.

CHAPTER TWENTY-THREE

LESA

LESA, pronounced "Lisa" stands for *Life Expectancy Set Aside*. LESA was born out of the financial overhaul of reverse mortgages and is a component of the financial assessment, which became effective March 2, 2015.[34] LESAs are not required in all HECMs; in fact, I believe less than 10% of reverse mortgages that have closed since the inception of the financial assessment have LESAs. So, what are they and how do they work?

Think of LESAs as a "forced escrow" or "forced savings" account (although they are not held in an actual escrow account). They are a calculated amount of equity that is set aside to pay for future property taxes, hazard insurance premiums and, if applicable, flood insurance premiums. They can be "fully" funded or "partially" funded, (I'll explain this in a minute), not required, or a borrower can request one. If the borrower requests a LESA, it must be fully funded.

So why would you need a LESA on your reverse mortgage? The reason is one of two. Remember from Chapter 16 our willingness and capacity conversations? Capacity and willingness are functions of the financial assessment. Do you have the capacity, or income, to pay your bills on time? Granted, life shows up and there are underwriting guidelines for LESAs, so know if one is needed it isn't the lender or underwriter making it up, as *all lenders follow the same rulebook: the HUD / FHA HECM underwriting guidelines.*

---

[34] HUD Mortgagee Letter 2014-21

That said, if a person has had or does have credit issues, it doesn't mean an automatic LESA. Credit issues most often reflect a life event causing a loss of income. Life shows up and some of those things in life that show up are called *extenuating circumstances*[35]. And if a borrower can "verify and document" an extenuating circumstance, a LESA may not be required. Verify and document is critical. It means show me the documents that support your story—the event that happened in your life.

An extenuating circumstance has specific rules that I am only going to highlight. Basically, it is defined as an economic event that causes the loss of at least 20% of a person's (or household's) income, lasts for at least six months, and *this is the critical part that most people don't know,* there is a re-establishment of credit for at least 12 months. Major health issues represent an excellent example of an extenuating circumstance. No one plans on major health occurrences such as cancer, heart attack, or stroke, for example, and these events quite often are emotionally and financially devastating.

Additionally, remember in Chapter 16, the residual income test everyone must pass with a HECM? If a borrower is a little short (again, based on underwriting rules), the lender may require a LESA to pay for the homeowner's property taxes and homeowners insurance through a LESA, and this could make the difference between the homeowner getting the reverse mortgage or not.

There is your high-level LESA requirements for a capacity issue. Let's move onto LESAs with respect to a willingness issue. Remember, willingness is credit. Credit said

---

[35] HUD Mortgagee Letter 2013-26

differently is character. A homeowner may have a very good income or substantial assets, but they just don't pay their bills very well. Think of this, for example, in the context of not paying your property taxes on time. If property taxes are not paid over a long enough period, that debt can move in front of a first mortgage, your reverse mortgage. If the lender doesn't monitor the payment of your property taxes and misses the delinquency, you and the lender could end up losing the home! And if the payment of property taxes isn't in the hands of the lender via a LESA, they are relying on you to pay the property taxes on time for, hopefully, many years to come. So, if a homeowner has demonstrated a history of not paying their bills or not paying their bills on time, the lender has a valid reason to enforce a LESA.

Whether the LESA is "fully funded" or "partially funded" simply means how much money needs to be put into a LESA per a person's financial assessment as LESAs can't have too much money for the funding of future applicable property charges. Know that all underwriters have a specific, *have to adhere to* HUD/FHA worksheet that is in the financial assessment and determines how much funds are required to be put in the LESA. And this, in turn, determines if it is a fully or partially funded LESA.

A couple more notes on the LESAs. If a fully funded LESA is required, the HECM can be *either* the fixed rate product *or* the adjustable rate product. However, a partially funded LESA is only available for with the adjustable interest rate HECM.

A person has a LESA... now let's take it out many years. First, you will know how much money is put into your LESA account if you need one. Again, you don't pay interest and mortgage insurance on these funds *until they are used*. Then every year the lender is required to perform an analysis of your LESA account. If the funds in a LESA are depleted such that there are insufficient funds remaining (I will cover why that could happen next), the lender must give the borrower a 30-day notice in writing of this occurrence.

During the time you have a LESA on a *fully* funded LESA, the *lender* (or servicer of your loan) is responsible for the payment of all property charges for as long as there are sufficient funds in the LESA account to cover them. It works a little different with a partially funded LESA. With partially funded LESAs, the homeowner is responsible for paying the property charges, as the lender doesn't pay them directly like they do with a fully funded LESA.

But here is the key component on both fully and partially funded LESAs: LESAs are established on the *life expectancy of the youngest borrower*. But we are living longer and if the youngest borrower outlives their life expectancy, there won't be enough funds in their LESA. In such case, the borrower will have to start paying their own property charges. This is even more critical to note with a partially funded LESA because not as many funds are set aside in those.

A quick note regarding non-borrowing spouses (covered in Chapter 12) and LESAs: If the borrower passes away or a maturity event occurs, and the non-borrowing spouse is now in their deferral period, the LESA stops paying their property charges. The non-borrowing spouse must now start paying those.

The final option with LESAs is that the homeowner will want to elect to voluntarily establish one. Not a bad thing, if enough equity is in the home to fulfill their goal(s) with a HECM *and* voluntarily establish a LESA. If a LESA is established then a homeowner truly has no mortgage payments, as the HECM wipes out the principal and interest payment and the LESA wipes out the property charges. Keep in mind a LESA is not going to cover any association or planned unit development fees, nor any other special assessments. These still must be paid by the homeowner.

Voluntary LESAs can be utilized on both fixed and adjustable rate HECMs. But they must be fully funded (the underwriter is going to determine that amount).

LESAs, which again are part of financial assessment, have proven to be needed on a relatively small percentage of HECMs. Knowing they exist and what they are, you are educated in the basics of them such that if an underwriter required one on your loan, you would know why and what is paid. Also, if you qualify, you know you have the option to utilize one if you wanted your reverse mortgage to also pay your property charges.

CHAPTER TWENTY-FOUR

My Final Thoughts

Reverse Mortgage: A New Perspective. I truly hope I have delivered a new perspective to you through the sharing of the material I have in this book. I'm grateful you have invested your time in reading my book to educate yourself on the reverse mortgage of today, and in doing so gained a new perspective of reverse mortgages.

As I have said, I don't want nor to expect you to become a financial expert in reverse mortgages (that's my job). However, with this new knowledge and having this book as a reference tool, you are far better equipped to consider a reverse mortgage. Whether you are a senior homeowner, their family or friend, or a senior supporting professional, I hope that everyone will feel much more comfortable and confident in when and why to consider or suggest a reverse mortgage.

Remember, we are dealing with a unique financial product, a reverse mortgage, not to mention the Federal government regulates it. Can you say never ending regulation? Changes? Complications? The never-ending need for education of the product? And inside of this domain, I truly hope you can see why my belief of working with a reverse mortgage specialist is so strong.

I have seen and continue to see the difference that a reverse mortgage can make in a senior's life. And some of those stories I will never forget, as they touched my heart. Today's reverse mortgage isn't for everyone, but it is for a lot more people than currently have taken advantage of the product. With new knowledge that gives new perspectives, my hope is this book will serve to educate people in today's reverse mortgages and for years to come I will be able to share many more stories of senior homeowners who have touched me because of the good this product is doing.

GLOSSARY

HECMs have their own unique language and terms. I have composed a list of the key terms with their definitions as a reference to give better understanding to HECM loans.

- **Adjustable Rate HECM (HECM ARM):** This is the HECM utilizing an adjustable rate. There are two ARM programs to choose from: a monthly or an annually adjustable rate loan. As the name implies, the monthly ARM interest rate will adjust monthly, and the annual adjustable rate HECM will adjust annually. Adjustable rate mortgages are comprised of an index and a margin. The sum of the two will equal the interest rate paid.
- **Cap:** This is expressed as a percentage and is the "ceiling" on how high an interest rate can increase. For example, "2/5" would mean the interest rate could adjust up to 2% per year but not exceed 5% over the life of the loan. The interest rate caps will be found in the note.
- **Claim Amount:** The maximum claim amount is the *lesser of* the national lending limit, currently $679,650[36], or the appraised value of the home. It is the claim amount that the principal limit factor (remember, expressed as a percentage) is applied to in order to determine the principle limit.[37]
- **Expected Rate:** This is a rate that is used to determine the principal limit on the HECM loan. It is NOT the current interest rate. Currently, the expected rate equals the 10-year swap rate plus the

---

[36] As of January 1, 2018
[37] HUD Handbook 4235.1 Rev-1, (1-4A.)

lenders margin. With a fixed rate HECM, the expected rate and the interest rate are the same.

- **Federal Housing Administration (FHA):** This is an agency within the U.S. Department of Housing and Urban Development (HUD) that issues insurance or insures the HECM.
- **Fixed Rate HECM:** Just as the name implies, this is the fixed interest rate HECM product. The interest rate will never change over the life of the loan.
- **Forward Mortgage:** I use and define this in the broadest sense. It includes all Fannie Mae, Freddie Mac, VA, FHA, USDA, and HELOC loans whereby principal and interest are paid monthly, thereby reducing the principal balance monthly. Typically, these are 15- or 30-year term loans.
- **HECM:** A Federal Housing Administration (FHA) insured mortgage for borrowers at least 62 years old. They are designed to convert the equity in their homes into available equity to the senior homeowner in various ways.
- **HECM for Purchase (H4P):** Allows seniors age 62 or over to purchase a principal residence and obtain a reverse mortgage within a single transaction.
- **HECM to HECM Refinance:** The ability to refinance an existing HECM into a new HECM. As this is currently a very small percentage of the HECM business, I did not cover it. HUD has strict guidelines that must be met in order for a borrower to qualify for a HECM to HECM refinance.

- **HUD:** The U.S. Housing and Urban Development. A federal agency that oversees the FHA and other housing and community development programs.
- **Initial Disbursement Limit:** This is the amount of equity that is available to the homeowner. For fixed rate HECMs, this is the amount that is only available at closing. For HECM-ARMs, it is the amount available at closing or for the first year. But the initial disbursement is limited to 60% of the principal limit, or the mandatory obligation plus 10% of the principal limit.
- **Initial Mortgage Insurance Premium (IMIP):** This is the initial (at closing) amount of mortgage insurance the borrower must pay. It is also called the *up-front mortgage insurance premium.* As of October 2, 2017, this amount for all HECMs is 2% of the value of the home. FHA maintains a specific fund for HECM insurance known as the Mutual Mortgage Insurance (MMI) Fund.
- **LIBOR (LIBOR Index):** This is the current index used in the adjustable rate HECM. This index plus the margin equals the interest rate being charged. It is an acronym and stands for London Interbank Offered Rate. While there are several LIBOR indexes, for the HECM product the 1-month or the 1-year index is used.
- **Line of Credit (LOC):** This feature is *only* available with the HECM-ARM program. Should a borrower have enough equity, a line of credit may be established. Funds that are available in the line of credit will grow monthly, regardless of the value of the home. Additionally, they will then be available for future use. These funds do not accrue interest

nor is mortgage insurance charged unless the funds are utilized.

- **Mandatory Obligations:** These are specific items that must be paid off at closing and include existing mortgage(s), liens, judgments that affect the property's title, federal debt, closing costs, initial mortgage insurance, and possibly the settlement of a divorce.
- **Margin:** Utilized only in the HECM-ARM, the margin is the percentage added to the index to then equal the interest rate. The margin is the constant in the interest rate, as it will never change for the life of the loan.
- **Maturity Events:** After a HECM closes, a borrower has responsibilities to uphold. This includes, but isn't limited to, living in the home as their primary residence, maintaining the home including the physical structure, and paying the real estate taxes, homeowner's insurance, flood insurance, and association fees if applicable. If violated, these contractual obligations would be cause for the mortgagee to foreclose on the loan.
- **Maximum Claim Amount (MCA):** The lesser of the home's appraised value or the HECM lending limit, which currently is $679,650[38]. Borrowers may still obtain a HECM on a home valued at greater than the MCA, however, the available funds will be calculated as though the home were valued at $679,650.
- **Modified Tenure:** Combining a tenure payment with a line of credit.

---

[38] As of January 1, 2018

- **Mortgage Insurance Premium (MIP):** In addition to the IMIP, HECMs require monthly mortgage insurance premiums be paid. These premiums are, with the IMIP, paid into the MMI fund maintained by FHA.
- **Mortgagee:** This is the lender in a mortgage transaction.
- **Mortgagor:** This is the borrower in a mortgage transaction.
- **Non-Borrowing Spouse (NBS):** Borrowers need to be 62 to obtain a reverse mortgage. Non-borrowing spouses are not 62, they are NOT on the loan or mortgage, but are on the title of the home. However, as of August 4, 2014, non-borrowing spouses have additional rights. They may be able to stay in the home as long as certain requirements are met.
- **Non-Recourse Feature:** The HECM is a non-recourse loan. This means that the HECM borrower (or his or her estate) will never owe more than the loan balance or value of the property, whichever is less: and no assets other than the home must be used to repay the debt[39].
- **Origination Fee:** This is a one-time fee that *may* be collected from your lender to compensate the lender for processing your HECM loan. The maximum origination fee is 2% of the initial $200,000 home value, and 1% on the home value thereafter up to $6,000. $6,000 is the maximum origination fee that can be charged, regardless of the value of the home.

---

[39] HUD Mortgagee letter 2008-38

- **Primary Residence:** A residence that will be occupied by the borrower for the majority of the calendar year.[40]
- **Principal Limit Factor (PLF):** The PLF is determined by the age of the youngest borrower (including non-borrowing spouse) and the expected rate (ER). HUD publishes PLF tables to determine how much the lender can offer the homeowner. PLFs are expressed as a percentage and applied to the value of the home. For example, a PLF of 60.6% would mean the borrower could obtain a HECM loan for 60.6% of the appraised value, or maximum claim amount, the lower of the two, of the home.
- **Principal Limit (PL):** Principal limits are expressed in dollars and represent the maximum dollar amount that can borrowed.
- **Reverse Mortgage:** The more commonly used name for HECMs. See HECM for definition.
- **Tenure Payment:** The borrower will receive equal monthly payments for as long as the borrower continues to occupy the property as their principal residence and not trip any maturity events.
- **Term Payment:** The borrower will receive equal monthly payments for a fixed period of months selected by the borrower, and as long as the borrower continues to occupy the property as their principal residence and not trip any maturity events.

---

[40] HUD Handbook 4155.1 Chapter 4, Section B

Made in the USA
Columbia, SC
20 July 2018